CAPITAL AND LANGUAGE

SEMIOTEXT(E) FOREIGN AGENTS SERIES

© 2008 Semiotext(e)
© 2002 DeriveApprodi

Published by Semiotext(e)
PO Box 629, South Pasadena, CA 91031
www.semiotexte.com

Special thanks to Robert Dewhurst for copyediting.

Cover art by Claire Fontaine
In God They Trust, 2005 (1966, A.P.)
Twenty-five cent coin, stainless box-cutter blade, solder and rivet.
Courtesy the artist and Reena Spaulings Fine Art, NY
Back Cover Photography by Marco Dotti
Design by Hedi El Kholti

ISBN: 978-1-58435-067-5 (pb : alk. paper)
Distributed by The MIT Press, Cambridge, Mass. and London, England

The MIT Press is pleased to keep this title available in print by manufacturing single copies, on demand, via digital printing technology.

CAPITAL AND LANGUAGE

FROM THE NEW ECONOMY TO THE WAR ECONOMY

Christian Marazzi

Introduction by Michael Hardt

Translated by Gregory Conti

\<e\>

Contents

Introduction: Language at Work   7

1. From Post-Fordism to the New Economy   13

2. The New Business Cycle   69

3. The Return of Surplus Value   101

4. War and the Business Cycle   145

Bibliography   159

Language at Work

Capital and Language is the first of Christian Marazzi's books to appear in English, and it is long overdue. A native of Ticino, the Italian canton of Switzerland, Marazzi got interested very early in Italian Workerism and participated actively to the Autonomia movement in Italy in the 1970s. After finishing his doctorate at the London City University, he joined the University of Padova, where he became a close friend of Ferrucio Gambino, Luciano Ferrari Bravo, Sergio Bologna, and Toni Negri. In 1977, he taught Negri's classes at Padova before being forced in turn to leave Italy. For a few years he lived in New York, London, and Montreal, and contributed to giving the problematics of Italian Workerism a multinational dimension. Rare enough are those economists who can communicate to a general public the complexities of financial markets and economic policy. Christian Marazzi is of even a rarer breed of economist who is also able to engage and advance the most exciting veins of contemporary political and social theory, using these theoretical lenses to read economic developments and reflecting back on those theories with feet solidly planted on the economic terrain.

What is specific about his work is its creative engagement with the hypothesis developed by Autonomia and the "post-workerist" perspective: worker struggles precede and prefigure the successive restructurings of capital, and those restructurings provide new possibilities for worker power. Beginning in the 1990s Marazzi published a series of books analyzing the post-Fordist economy, that is, the economic condition, whose beginnings trace back to the 1970s, in which economic production in the dominant countries is no longer centered on the factory, labor processes are no longer governed by the Taylorist rationality and discipline typical of the assembly line, and Fordist wage relations no longer function as a guarantee of social reproduction. Marazzi focused specifically on two crucial areas of the so-called "New Economy": the financial sector, which has come to play an increasingly central and guiding role in the economy, and the newly dominant forms of social labor. The series began in 1995 with *Il posto dei calzini: la svolta linguistic dell'economia e i suoi effetti sulla politica* (*The Place for Socks: The Linguistic Turn of the Economy and its Political Effects*), and continued in 1998 with *E il denaro va: esodo e rivoluzione dei marcati finanziari* (*And So the Money Goes: Exodus and Revolution of the Financial Markets*). *Capital and Language*, published in 2002, his third book, is bringing together the first two.

The central thesis of *Capital and Language* is that language offers a model to understand the functioning and crises of the contemporary capitalist economy. This is really a double claim: 1)that the world of finance is characterized by and functions through linguistic conventions, and 2) that the newly dominant forms of labor are produced through language and means analogous to linguistic performance. Each of these claims is provocative and revealing, and what I find most fascinating, in fact, is the link between the two.

In order to understand his argument about finance, one first has to identify the two opposing standard views that Marazzi rejected. Finance is not, as some neoclassical and monetarist economists would have it, a realm of self-generating value, relatively autonomous from human labor and the production processes. It is not either, as some veins of Marxist and critical thought maintain, merely composed of fictive values and pure speculation, again relatively separate from the "real economy." Marazzi argues instead that we need a linguistic theory to understand the workings of contemporary finance markets. On the first, most banal level we can see that finance requires the constant communication of data and information. Marazzi concentrates, however, on a second level in which finance functions through linguistic conventions. Speech acts, such as a pronouncement by the Chair of the U.S. Federal Reserve, can have extraordinary, real effects on financial markets, but those effects are dependent on a speech community that shares a set of beliefs and linguistic conventions. A third level, the most intriguing in my eyes, is how the language of finance is linked to labor and production since it could open the path for a future politics.

Finance, like money in general, expresses the value of labor and the value produced by labor, but through highly abstract means. The specificity of finance, in some respects, is that it attempts to represent the future value of labor and its future productivity. In any case, analyzing how finance might be understood as an expression of labor in analogy with linguistic relations, and thereby grasping what kind of representation finance operates as, seems to me a promising and exciting idea.

The role of language in the newly dominant forms of labor and production is even more direct. Whereas factory labor was in many respects mute, as Paolo Virno says, the social labor outside the factory typical of post-Fordism is loquacious. Labor in service jobs, the media, health, education, and increasingly all other sectors of the economy is characterized by the centrality of language and linguistic capacities. Language and communication are crucial for the production of ideas, information, images, affects, social relationships, and the like. Marazzi analyzes how, as labor becomes increasingly defined by linguistic performance, worktime has generally increased and, in fact, the traditional barriers that divide work-time from nonworktime, that divide work from life, are progressively breaking down, a fact which carries with it a series of important consequences. Labor produces social life and, in turn, all of social life is put to work.

In one of the passages of his analysis that I find most suggestive, Marazzi revises Marx's notion of "General Intellect" in the context of contemporary capitalist production. Marx uses the term to indicate how knowledge, especially technical and scientific knowledge, has become a primary productive force and how that knowledge has been consolidated in machines as fixed capital. The power loom and the steam engine, like the computer and the cell phone, make concrete and productive volumes of accumulated socially produced scientific and cultural knowledges as General Intellect. Marx's view is correct, according to Marazzi, but limited because General Intellect and the productive force of knowledge reside not only in machines but also, and increasingly today, in linguistic communication and cooperation. One might say, working with Marx's categories, that our brains, linguistic faculties, and interactive skills have taken the place of fixed capital. Or, from a slightly different perspective, that this indicates the increasing autonomy of living labor from capitalist control, since, by embodying General Intellect, it is ever more independently able to deploy and manage the productive forces of knowledge and language.

At this point we can take a step back to grasp the significance of the parallel that Marazzi articulates between finance and post-Fordist labor, both of which function primarily through linguistic means. This recognition could provide us with a basis for exploring how financialization and financial mechanisms, rather than the disciplinary tools available to the industrial capitalist, are increasingly becoming today the primary means to control labor and social production in general. In this book Marazzi examines the other side of the equation. Is it possible to read the liquidity, communication, and future orientation of financial markets as a prefiguration—albeit an inverted, distorted, corrupted prefiguration—of the liberation of the multitude? Posing that question highlights the potential freedom of social cooperation in the multitude, the potential autonomy from capitalist control of the linguistic performance, knowledge production, and capacities of communication and cooperation of contemporary living labor. What Marazzi suggests here is that while combating financial control we can also study the way it functions through language and linguistic conventions, thereby advancing our understanding of the productive capacities of the multitude and its potential autonomy from capital.

— Michael Hardt

1

From Post-Fordism to the New Economy

Introduction

First of all, let's try to sketch the broad outlines of the historical framework within which the transition from post-Fordism to the New Economy has played itself out. Although the distinction between post-Fordism and the New Economy is probably improper, given that practically all the constitutive elements of the so-called post-Fordist paradigm are also present in the New Economy, the distinction is nevertheless useful for us because it allows us to highlight a diversity of analytical approaches in the interpretation of the great transformation of the system of capitalist accumulation that has come about over the last twenty years. If in fact, beginning in the second half of the 1980s, the prevailing analyses of the crisis of Fordism and the transition to post-Fordism were based in socio-economics, with particular attention to modifications in the nature of work and the production of goods, starting in the second half of the 1990s the explosion of the securities markets on a global scale forced almost everyone to "update" their analyses by paying more attention to the financial dimension of the *paradigmatic shift*. It is no coincidence that, even today, the greatest difficulty lies in "holding together," in a relationship of reciprocal and dialectic functionality, the elements which emerged in the first phase of the study of post-Fordism and the factors characteristic of the financialization of the capitalist economy which emerged in the second stage of inquiry into the New Economy. As we shall see in the course of our discussion, there is often a strong temptation to describe the performance of the securities markets, and the extreme volatility which has characterized them over the past several years, as the expression of the separation of financial capital from real economic processes that was so typical of the terminal phase of the industrial *business cycle* in the 19th and 20th centuries. To my way of thinking, in the post-Fordist New Economy the distinction between the real economy, in which material and immaterial goods are produced and sold, and the monetary-financial economy, where the speculative dimension dominates investor decisions, must be totally reconceived. The thesis I wish to demonstrate here is that in the New Economy *language* and communication are structurally and contemporaneously present throughout both the sphere of the production and distribution of goods and services and the sphere of finance, and that it is for *this very reason* that changes in the world of work and modifications in the financial markets must be seen as two sides of the same coin.

Historical Roots

Federico Rampini, who as West Coast correspondent for the Rome daily "La Repubblica," had the opportunity to observe the crisis of the New Economy from a front row seat, begins his retrospective analysis like this: "Because of a singular disconnect between the real economy and finance, the year 2000 was at one and the same time the last year of the great magic spell and the first year of brutal disillusionment. The world economy grew by 5%, the strongest growth rate in the last 16 years, still driven by an American economy in perfect health: 4% unemployment, the lowest since the Vietnam War. But in the meantime, Wall Street was already heading toward collapse. For the stock market, the depression had begun in March of that year. The crash in stock prices was so unexpected and so violent that at the end of 2000 American investors discovered, for the first time in 55 years, which is to say, from the time we have had reliable statistics on family wealth, that they were actually poorer" (Rampini, 2001).

The moment of crisis, Rampini rightly emphasizes, is the moment when historical memory, the recollection of the great crises of the past, comes to the fore. All of a sudden, for example, the realization dawns that "the 1920s had also witnessed a New Economy that had given rise to great innovations and changed the face of modern industry: the advent of the automobile, the widespread availability of electrical energy, the invention of cinema. But when the crash came, between 1929 and 1932, Wall Street lost 90% of its capitalization."

Actually, in making comparisons with historical crises and the expansive phases that preceded them, the differences count more than the similarities. And one decidedly important difference is that today 60% of American families have investments in the stock market either directly or indirectly through pension funds and mutual funds (in 1989 the figure was less than 30%). Another peculiarity of the New Economy is that what drove the expansive phase of financial markets to the point of collapse were tech stocks, that is, shares in that combination of information technologies that have sent the labor market into turmoil, upsetting all the basic tenets of the Fordist model of production. In other words, new technologies and financialization on a massive social scale are the two extremes from which we must begin to identify the historical trajectories along which the cycle, and the crisis, of the New Economy have been forged.

"For some time now," writes Marco Magrini in *La richezza digitale*, "the financial markets have been electronic, even though just a few years ago only the professionals could afford the expensive equipment involved in electronic securities trading. But with the advent of the internet and the on-line debut of *discount brokers* (many of whom began in the 1970s with the law deregulating brokerage commissions) digital investing has become available to everyone" (Magrini, 1999, p.18).

In 1975 the United States initiated the process of multiplying the devices for draining off savings in order to reinforce stock-market financing of the economy. Thanks to the deregulation of brokerage commissions, which up to that time had been fixed with no possibility for discounting, new brokerage companies (*discount brokers*) were allowed to compete on commissions to attract investors. Deregulation broke the monopoly on the manipulation of share prices previously held by the large institutions which "make the market" (such as Goldman Sachs, Salomon Brothers, Morgan Stanley), by the institutions that controlled electronic access to the securities markets (the *wire houses* like Merrill Lynch, Smith Barney, Prudential), all the way down to the monopoly of local savings held by small regional banks.

It is in the second half of the 1970s, then, that the massification of stock market investment, what we might call the "socialization of finance," begins to take shape, and over the course of the 1990s, with the explosion of the internet and *online trading*, it would increase dramatically.

The computerization of raising funds and their placement on the securities markets, therefore, *follows* a structural change that happened *first*, a process that has its origin in the 1974–75 *fiscal crisis* of the welfare state in New York as a crisis of political control over social welfare spending, a crisis of the transformation into a salaried workforce of the manual laborers flowing into the rich urban centers from the poor racist states of the American South. The famous book by Paul Drucker, with the even more significant title, *the Unseen Revolution: How Pension Fund Socialism Came to America*, was published in 1976! The silent pension fund revolution that Drucker talks about got its start in the use of public employee pension funds to finance New York City's deficit, thus avoiding raising taxes on the rich, always ready to threaten the local authorities with moving their business elsewhere. This coinvolvement of public employees in the reinforcement of the city's financial discipline, under pain of reducing returns on pension funds invested in *city bonds* (an operation made possible by the unions that moved in to replace investors frightened off by New York's social and financial crisis), nullified any possibility of forming a political alliance between the new urban poor and the public officials charged with the management of social welfare programs, officials who were themselves caught up in the restructuring and rationalizing the public administration.

The deregulation of brokerage commissions in 1975, which, with *discount brokers* and, later on, *online traders*, who would then be followed by today's *microtraders*, favored the massive raising and diverting of funds into securities, was thus symmetrical to the use of pension funds to finance public deficits. These are the years which saw the start of the rearticulation of state and entrepreneurial power over the naked lives of the urban proletariat. The new power began by making the *public sphere* act against the particularities of the proletariat, against the *demand for life* of the unemployed at a time when the occupational crisis of the wage labor market was taking shape. By tying savings to the future yields of government bonds, the power of command over the public sector is exercised in the obligatory deferment of the right to live, "here and now," a decent life.

The second constitutive moment of the New Economy came in October 1979 with the decision of then Chairman of the Federal Reserve, Paul Volker, to use Friedmanesque measures of monetary policy to attack both domestic inflation in the United States (the monetary expression of the "explosion of wages and salaries" and of the effects of the oil crisis of 1974), and the international devaluation of the dollar (the reflection of the loss of US control over the global money supply and international credit flows).

Giovanni Arrighi, who in the fourth chapter of his *The Long Twentieth Century* provides a precise reconstruction of the dynamics leading up to the monetarist turn of 1979, writes: "US monetary policies in the 1970s were instead attempting to entice capital to keep the material expansion of the US-centered capitalist world-economy going, notwithstanding the fact that such an expansion had become the primary cause of rising costs, risks, and uncertainty for corporate capital in general and US corporate capital in particular. Not surprisingly, only a fraction of the liquidity created by the US monetary authorities found its way into new trade and production facilities. Most of it turned into petrodollars and Eurodollars, which reproduced themselves many times over through the mechanisms of private interbank money creation as competitors of the dollars issued by the US government" (Arrighi, 1994, p. 314).

The monetarist shift, which would be followed by a series of market liberalization measures, by the privatization of public resources, and by financialization on a global scale, is not directly connected with Reaganite or Thatcherite neoliberal ideology, but with the politico-economic crisis of the international Fordist model. "In 1978 the government of the United States"—writes Arrighi—"was faced with a choice between bringing the confrontation with the cosmopolitan financial community that controlled the Eurocurrency market to a decisive rendering of accounts by persevering in its own expansive monetary policies, or trying instead to reach an agreement by way of a stricter adherence to the principles and practice of currency stability. In the end, capitalist rationality prevailed. Starting in the last year of the Carter presidency, and with greater determination under the Reagan administration, the U.S. government opted for the second line of conduct. And when a new 'memorable alliance' was signed between the power of the State and the power of capital, the expansive monetary policies of the United States, which had characterized the entire Cold War era, gave way to policies that were extremely restrictive."

The dramatic increase in interest rates had immediate and long-term consequences on public and private sector debt, forcing capital to depend more and more on stock markets for its own financing and, therefore, to depend on the flow of savings into those same markets.

Not coincidetally, it was 1981 that saw the first defined-*contribution* pension plan, the 401(k) program, which, differently from earlier defined-*benefit* plans, makes pension fund benefits dependent on returns from the securities in which the funds are invested. "Labor unions," writes Robert Shiller in *Irrational Exuberance*

(2000), "have traditionally sought defined benefit plans for their members as a way of ensuring their welfare in retirement, and the decline of unions has meant diminishing support for these plans. The importance of the manufacturing sector, long a stronghold of labor unions and defined benefit pensions, has shrunk" (Shiller, 2000, p.32).

Since the 1950s, Wall Street had been trying, without much success, to foster interest in the securities markets, but, as Shiller writes, "no set of seminars that the exchange could ever afford could compare with the learning by-doing effects of the defined contribution plan in encouraging public knowledge about and interest in stocks" (Shiller, 2000, p.33). Although the objective of such funds is to encourage investors to take the long-term view in order to prepare them for retirement, defined-contribution plans are structured in such a way as to favor stocks over bonds and real estate, and this is made possible by the fact that people tend to distribute their funds, that is, their savings, in an unbalanced way across the various options, without taking into consideration the content of the preselected options. In this way, the *value of interest* or of *curiosity* for stocks has the better over any individual decision-making rationality, over any attention for what *concretely* and specifically stands behind securities listed on the stock exchange, over any *individual belief.*

Part of the reason for the success of *mutual funds*—the other collective fund-raising instrument which between 1982, the first year of the market rally that would later be associated with the takeoff of the New Economy, and the late 1990s, saw the number of American holders of mutual fund investment units increase from 6.2 million to 120 million, or about 2 units per family—must be attributed to their use as part of 401(k) pension plans. By first becoming familiar with investing in securities for pension purposes, people ended up investing even their nonretirement savings in mutual funds. Equally important for the growth of mutual funds was the publicity that they were given on television shows, magazines, and newspapers. From the early 1980s to the late 1990s open-end funds increased in tandem with the reduction in the inflation rate and the barrage of mass media advertising aimed at the least expert and most unwary investors.

The onset of pension funds and mutual funds began the draining of collective savings, first in America and then around the world, and their increasing investment in securities. What we call *financialization* is the diversion of savings from household economies to stocks and securities which, as part of the trend shifting the financing of the economy from the banking sector to the securities sector, contributed decisively to the formation of the end-of-millennium New Economy.

The Sovereignty of Public Opinion

The historical development of the New Economy demonstrates the important role of the means of mass communication in creating a favorable environment for the stock market. Indeed, in order for it to work, financialization depends on *mimetic rationality*, a kind of herd behavior based on the information deficit of individual investors.

We will have to devote some time to this question because it is decisive for the historical reconstruction of the New Economy. We have already said, in relation to the "silent revolution" of pension funds at the time of New York's fiscal crisis, that the investment of collective savings in securities markets ends up determining the exercise of the power of public opinion over individual destinies. In the name of his interests as a *shareholder* the *salaried* employee (in the public or private sector) is prepared to fire himself if Wall Street should demand it.

In order to account for this paradoxical anthropological meta-morphosis of the postmodern citizen (almost to the level of mass self-affliction), and to explain the immense increase in financial flows (today for every dollar of goods exchanged there are 55 dollars of financial assets in circulation), we must have a *theory of finance* in step with the times. Thanks to experts in the science of *behavioral finance* like Robert Shiller (2000) or Hersh Shefrin (2000), over the last 15 years we have seen a gradual withdrawal from the amazingly diehard neoclassical assumption according to which all people are perfectly rational and maximizing, such that the performance of securities listed on the stock exchanges are a "complete synthesis" of all financial information. The theorists of behavioral finance, on the other hand, try to incorporate some elements that may characterize human behavior from a *psychological* point of view.

"Most investors," Shiller writes, "also seem to view the stock market as a force of nature unto itself. They do not fully realize that they themselves, as a group, determine the level of the market. And they underestimate how similar to their own thinking is that of other investors. Many individual investors think that institutional investors dominate the market and that these 'smart money' investors have sophisticated models to understand prices, superior knowledge. Little do they know that most institutional investors are, by and large, equally clueless about the level of the market. In short, the price level is driven to a certain extent by a self-fulfilling prophecy based on similar hunches held by a vast cross section of large and small investors and reinforced by news media that are often content to ratify this investor-induced conventional wisdom" (Shiller p. xv).

One important result of the empirical studies of the behavioral finance theorists is this very notion of *imitative behavior* based on the *structural information deficits* of all investors, be they large or small. The final share price is the product of "self-fulfilling prophecies," and thus has little or nothing to do with the real economic value of the asset that the stock certificate represents. The modalities of communication of what the "others" consider a good stock to invest in counts more than what is communicated.

"The media were a fundamental mechanism in the financial bubble of the New Economy. They exalted the 'irrational exuberance' of the markets, feeding the herd behavior that, at a certain point, came to be theorized as a sophisticated financial technique: *momentum financing*. What does that mean? That to make money on the stock market you didn't need to waste time analyzing the listed companies; you had to make a timely guess as to what stocks the herd would be rushing to, ride the wave, cash in on the inevitable rise. For *momentum investing* the role of information was fundamental. And this naturally damaged the image of the transparent market, of all those informed and independent investors, so dear to the neoclassical economists" (Rampini, 2001, p.14).

The French economist André Orléan (1999) has pushed the critique of neoclassical finance even further than the behavioral theorists. In the wake of the teachings of J.M. Keynes (with particular reference to Chapter 12 of the *General Theory*) and on the basis of the experience of actual market operators like George Soros and Pierre Balley, Orléan submits that it is in the *nature itself* of financial markets to function on the basis of the herd behavior of the mass of investors, and that is why *communication* is a fundamental ingredient of markets.

At odds with those who believe that "the minute by minute television coverage of Wall Street distorts the workings of the market, transforming a group of thinking investors into a herd that thinks as a single animal: sell or buy, all together" (James Surowiecki), Orléan demonstrates how the mimetic behavior of investors is not a value-distorting factor. The herd behavior that reveals itself through the acceptance by millions of investors of symbols and signs that each of them recognizes as the legitimate expression of wealth, is instead *intrinsic* to the concept, so central in financial markets, of *liquidity*.

Liquidity, even prior to its being a concrete monetary function, is a concept. It arises from the need for securities in which people have invested their savings to be rapidly exchangeable. If securities were not liquid, that is to say *negotiable*, the propensity to invest would be strongly inhibited (in the case of an urgent need of liquidity, those who have invested their savings in the stock exchange and who cannot sell the securities in which they have invested those savings, are headed for certain bankruptcy). "The objective," Orléan writes, "is to transform what amounts to a personal wager on future dividends into immediate wealth here and now. To this end, it is necessary to transform individual, subjective evaluations into a price everyone can accept. Put another way, liquidity requires the production of a reference value that tells all financiers the price at which the security can be exchanged. The social structure which permits the attainment of such a result is the market: *the financial market organizes the confrontation between the personal opinions of investors in such a way as to produce a collective judgment that has the status of a reference value*. The figure that emerges in this manner has the nature of a consensus that crystallizes the agreement of the financial community. Announced publicly, it has the value of a norm: it is the price at which the market agrees to sell and buy the security in question, at a certain moment. That is how the security is made liquid. The financial market, because it institutes collective opinion as the reference norm, produces an evaluation of the security unanimously recognized by the financial community" (Orléan, 1999, pp. 31-32).

We will examine the contradictions in the liquidity of financial markets (the "paradox of liquidity") when we analyze the crisis of the New Economy. For the moment, we need only observe that liquidity is the product of an *institutional invention*, an indispensable product that enables markets to function in their capacity as capital attractors, as places where collective savings are invested for the financing of enterprises. Furthermore, liquidity seen as the result of the (rather complicated) architecture of financial markets leads to consideration of *speculation* as the fruit of market operations, a constriction on all investors deriving from the supremacy of "market psychology" (of collective opinion) over individual opinions and beliefs. I may be absolutely certain that there is no danger of inflation, but if the Chairman of the Federal Reserve says, for example, that the labor market is stretched thin, it is clear that I will adapt myself to his "prophecy" ("wages will rise and therefore prices will also rise …"). If I don't want my stocks to lose value, I respond to Greenspan's declaration by selling as soon as possible because, certainly, everyone, sure that Greenspan is going to raise the interest rate, will do likewise ("everyone" except the skeptics who speculate on the marginal fluctuations *around* conventionally predictable trends, and the *contrarians*, who speculate *against* the market, against the conventional wisdom, and who consequently are the most dangerous). To make profits, or to not lose money, it is not necessary to have the right opinion but to succeed in predicting how the market is going to move. It rarely happens that you can beat the herd, even though some do.

On the financial markets speculative behavior is *rational* because the markets are *self-referential*. Prices are the expression of the action of collective opinion, the individual investor does not react to information but to what he believes will be the reaction of the other investors in the face of that information. It follows that the values of securities listed on the stock exchange make reference to themselves and not to their underlying economic value. This is the self-referential nature of the markets, in which the *disassociation* between economic value and exchange value is symmetrical to the disassociation between individual belief and collective belief.

"There is no reality independent of subjective bias," George Soros writes about the reflexivity of markets, "but there is a reality that is influenced by it. In other words, there is a sequence of events which actually happens, and this sequence incorporates the effect of the participants' biases. It is likely, that is, that the actual course of events differs from the expectations of the participants, and the divergence can be assumed as an indication of the distortion that comes into play. Unfortunately, it only serves as an indication—not as a measure of the full bias—because the actual course of events already incorporates the effects of the participants' bias. A phenomenon that is partially observable and partially submerged in the course of events is of limited value as an instrument of scientific investigation. We can now appreciate why economists were so anxious to eliminate it from their universe. I, on the other hand, consider it the key to understanding financial markets. The course of events that participants in financial markets try to anticipate consists of market prices. These are readily observable, but they do not, by themselves, reveal anything about the participant's bias. To identify the bias we need some other variable that is not contaminated by the bias. The conventional interpretation of financial markets posits such a variable: it consists of the fundamentals that market prices are supposed to reflect" (Soros, 1998, p.48).

It all comes down to understanding how this "other variable" that Soros refers to, comes to be created: the dominant interpretive model (my/our being sure that Greenspan is going to raise interest rates), the *convention*, as Keynes calls the opinion that in a certain period has the upper hand over the multiplicity of opinions and that, as the "elect" of the community, becomes *public opinion*. What is the interpretive model of the "facts" and how does it become dominant? How does it acquire the legitimacy that allows it to determine the actions of the multiplicity of players participating in the economic and financial game? When and how does a convention thought to be stable, almost a fact of nature, come to collapse? This is what we want to understand by studying the New Economy.

Pathways of Language Analysis

The theoretical analysis of financial market operations reveals the centrality of communication, of *language*, not only as a vehicle for transmitting data and information, but also as a *creative force*. Communicative action is at the origin of the conventions, of the "interpretive models" that influence the choices and the decisions of the multitude of players operating in the markets. For companies listed on the stock exchange, the centrality of communication certainly leads to economic distortions, in that the self-referentiality of the markets exposes them to the volatility risks of the markets originating from factors—and it is sufficient to recall the pressure exerted by shareholders on company management—which have little or nothing to do with productive rationality.

It must be understood, however, that a convention (for example, in the 1990s an average return of 15% on capital invested in securities became an outright convention) is not right or wrong by virtue of its being a good or bad representation of objective reality, but by virtue of its public force. It is the *public* nature of conventions that must be explained because it is on *this* basis that financial markets work.

In Keynesian terms, "The concept of the self-fulfilling prophecy breaks with this [ed. note: the neoclassical theory of prices based on the scarcity of goods] naturalist epistemology. It proposes a radically new idea: beliefs have a creative role. What the actors think, the way they represent the world, has an effect on prices and, therefore, on the relationships that economic actors weave among themselves. This conception profoundly alters our analysis of the crisis and of the ways for overcoming it. For Keynes, the obstacle to full employment is not the objective scarcity of capital, but the way in which individuals represent to themselves the normal value of the interest rate. They believe in a value that's too high to permit full employment. The obstacles between people and their happiness are no longer exogenous natural constrictions but their own beliefs" (Orléan, 1999, p. 85).

The conventions work and, historically, they change because they act as *cognitive constrictions* on the multiplicity of players operating on the markets. The recurrence of conventions over the course of certain historic periods is such that it almost always happens that their *conventional* nature is forgotten, so that most people end up believing them to be conventions rooted in the *nature* of things.

This function of conventions is eminently *linguistic*. And it is such *even before* it is psychological. Here lies, by the way, the limitation of behavioral finance theory. In order to explain the workings of financial markets in the era of post-Fordism what we need is a *linguistic theory* of their operations.

I would like to suggest, in a necessarily very schematic and very personal way, three levels or pathways of language analysis that allow us to comprehend some fundamental aspects of the workings of financial markets.

Language and Body

The first level concerns language analysis from the point of view of its *biological foundation*. I allude to the work in the philosophy of language by Felice Ciamatti and to the theory of the oncologist Giorgio Prodi, which Ciamatti himself brought to my attention (see Ciamatti, 2000b).

For biological theory, "language is neither historical, because man certainly didn't invent language, nor simply natural, because it is equally true that without the participation of the human animal, our language wouldn't exist" (*ibid.* p. 80). In our past there is "no moment in which there was a man without language who decided to invent one. That hypothetical man without language, but in all other respects similar to us, never existed. The human animal is what it is because it literally constructed itself around language."

The relational nature of language, that is, that one *learns* how to use language, and one learns it from/with someone else, does not mean, however, that language is only an arbitrary social institution, and that is because language is subject to very strong *genetic restraints*. If linguistic intermediation works, says Prodi, it is because man's brain is made in the right way: "in fact our language cannot be taught (beyond the most minimal and insignificant fraction) to nonhuman animals, even to those that are in certain ways very intelligent; nor, by the same token, can a human animal, once beyond a certain age, learn to talk."

Not only are we human animals to the extent that we are linguistic animals; not only, that is, is the linguisticity of our being (the fact that the peculiarity of man is to talk) what differentiates us from non-human animals (cf. Ciamatti, 2000a): "*the environment of the human animal is language itself*; the human animal is adapted to language, is made *for and by* language."

Body and language, therefore. Language faculty *and* neuronal resources. In this theory of language, there is no distinction whatsoever between intention and instrument: "This is an untenable distinction because, in the evolutionary history of language, there is no intention which precedes the instrument." The duality between intention and language, according to which language began because, first, there was a "desire" for language, simply does not exist. There is instead *circularity* between intention and language ("in this case it is, if anything, the instrument—language—that has molded its user").

The biological theory of language has this especially innovative feature: it explains how the language faculty, the fact of talking, *is one and the same with our bodies*. Our language faculty developed *physically/physiologically* (in *nature*) inside the phenomena of *life*, right from our very first proto-semiotic interactions.

Language and Difference

The biological (natural, if you will) dimension of language, the dimension that defines our ability to talk, while it characterizes the species-specificity of humans (the fact that *all* members of the human species have this language faculty), must then be analyzed from the point of view of *linguistic difference*, and in the first place of gender difference. The insertion of difference into language analysis begins with the political reflections of women on the symbolic organization of society: how to be "inside and against" language when the linguistic organization of society, its operation, is patriarchal.

At this second level, difference arises in the passage (the so-called "thetic cut") from the intrauterine semiotic sphere to the social symbolic sphere, from communication inside the mother's womb to the completely symbolic language of the historically determined world. "The life we live before knowing how to talk must be seen as life lived in learning how to talk." We learn to talk from our mother and this initiation to language defines us as beings-in-relation, ontologically linguistic beings, but, at the same time, beings capable of distinguishing "who is the mother/what is language" (see Muraro, 1991).

The work of Alfred Tommatis allows us to understand that at the origin of language there is a precise *need of communication*, and it is this same need that makes us human animals not only linguistic animals but also animals capable of distinguishing different symbolic levels. The need to communicate "arises first of all from the desire not to break (or eventually to renew) the sonic relationship with the mother during prenatal life. The human being wants to conserve or reestablish a bond with the outside world and with the other world from which he drew, when still in the embryonic phase, the greatest satisfaction" (Tommatis, 1977, p. 248).

Verbal dialogue, as *dialogue between fleshy beings* initiated by the human embryo with the first Other who is the mother, does not vanish at birth and entry into the world of abstract/symbolic language, but is maintained (is immanentized) as a *faculty* of difference. The physical perception of language as the "play of sounds" ("language too," Tommatis says, "possesses a physical dimension. Provoking a kind of vibration in the surrounding air, it becomes a sort of invisible member, thanks to which we can *touch*, in the fullest sense of the word, him who listens to us"), if on the one hand it finds in the language of the father its first obstacle (the other as the first stranger who speaks the language of society), on the other hand, it fixes definitively (ontologically) the faculty of difference *inside* language itself, within the same symbolic (metaphoric) pervasiveness of which extrauterine language is capable.

In its, if you will, carnal dimension, language defines what Jakobson called the *metonymic pole* of language, the pole that takes us linguistically back to things; the *metaphorical pole*, on the other hand, is the dimension that, by expanding the meaning of words, always risks transcending the physicality and the contextuality of language (that which, one could say, tries to distance us or finally separate us from the local "uterine" sphere) (see Muraro, 1998).

This is a very important point: intrauterine language defines us as beings-of-difference to the extent that we enter into historically determined language *with a body capable of distinguishing different symbolic levels*. Our body is born "in" language, "in" relation, in that linguistic relation in which the prime symbolic level is given as the *union* of life and language.

Language and Multitude

The third level of language analysis concerns what happens when the action of the faculty of difference "inside" symbolic language causes its wrapping to, we might say, explode (as when the passage from the maternal womb to the outside world causes the placenta to "explode").

By making reference to a category elaborated by John L. Austin (see his work with the exceedingly meaningful title, *How To Do Things With Words*, 1975), in the field of the philosophy of language, it can be submitted that a convention, that convention which we have seen acting on the financial markets, is the fruit of a series of performative utterances, that is, utterances which do not describe a state of things but which immediately *produce* real facts. If we consider language to be not only an instrument used in institutional reality to *describe* facts, but also to *create them*, then in a world in which institutions like money, property, marriage, technologies, work itself, are all *linguistic* institutions, what molds our consciousness, language, becomes at the same time an instrument of production of those same real facts. *Facts are created by speaking them.* "It is well known that John L. Austin defines as performative such utterances as 'I take this woman to be my lawfully wedded wife,' 'I baptize this baby Luke,' 'I swear I'll come to Rome,' 'I bet a thousand lire that Inter will win the championship,' etc. The speaker does not describe an action (a wedding, a baptism, an oath, a wager), he does it. He does not speak about what he is doing, but he does something by speaking" (Virno, 2001).

John Searle sees in today's money a demonstration of Austin's theory of performative utterances (Searle, 1985, p. 126–28). When the U.S. Treasury prints on a twenty dollar bill, "This bill is legal tender for all public and private debts," it is not merely describing a fact, it is, in reality, *creating* one. A performative utterance is one in which saying something makes that something true.

To the extent we use the term X to represent the state/function Y, we use X symbolically, we use it as a linguistic device. When, however, the term X has *no* physical support to which it linguistically refers, the linguistic act (saying X) becomes a productive act "in itself," *constitutive of the function Y*. For "chair" and "knife" the function of their use is written in the physicality of the chair and the knife. But for "money," "I take this woman as my lawfully wedded wife," or for securities on the Nasdaq, there is no physical support in which these states/functions are concretized. The linguistic-communicative act is constitutive of the money, the marriage, and even of the *Dot Com* enterprise, of which the shares I have purchased represent a portion of the share capital that allows the company to function economically.

In order for each person to see the conventional model of interpretation as the "true" model of reality, without therefore radically calling into question its pertinence, it is necessary that the performativeness of the convention derive its legitimacy from its being relatively external/autonomous with respect to the multiplicity of individual beliefs. The efficacy of performative language, as Emile Benveniste has said, depends on the legitimacy of the person who utters it; depends, that is, on the *power* and the *legal* status of the speaker. There is a big difference if the person who says that the markets are prey to some form of irrational exuberance is Alan Greenspan or the present writer.

The plot thickens when *even* Alan Greespan, although speaking from the heights of his authority, no longer manages to modify the current state of affairs, for example when, announcing a reduction in interest rates, he fails to convince the community of investors of the real possibility of an economic recovery. In this case we are in a crisis situation, a crisis that highlights the kind of performativity that Virno has defined as the *absolute performative*. "While, 'I forgive you' or 'I order you to go' are events produced by language, 'I speak' gives rise exclusively to a *language event*."

For the purposes of our analysis, the absolute performative is an especially useful category of language theory because it is immediately applicable to the crisis of the financial markets as a crisis of the *overproduction of self-referentiality*. "With respect to ordinary performatives ('I swear I'll come to Rome,' 'I baptize this baby Luke,' etc.) 'I speak' is integrally self-referential. The ordinary performative mentions the action that is performed by way of its very utterance, but it makes no mention of the latter. The dark corner of the self-reflective movement is, in this case, the *fact-that-one speaks*. 'I take this woman as my lawfully wedded wife' refers to the reality produced *by* the saying or the not saying, not to the reality *of* the saying. 'I speak,' on the other hand, refers instead to its own utterance as the salient event which it produces by the mere fact of being uttered."

The crisis of the financial markets reveals the *bodiless* self-referentiality of financial language. The crisis of ordinary performatives reveals, instead, that the fact-that-one speaks can never be separated from a living body." In other words, the pure faculty of language (the absolute performative) is more universal, more powerful than the *langue financiere*. The self-referentiality of the markets undoubtedly demonstrates the efficacy of the performative, but it is an efficacy that presupposes the *negation* of the body of the speakers (for example, of the investors who have internalized the dominant financial convention). The self-referentiality of the absolute performative, on the other hand, *presupposes* the body of the speaker.

We have said that the process which, historically, leads to the fixing of a universally accepted convention is a process in which the multitude of economic actors becomes a community by selecting/electing a supraindividual convention in order to turn it into an interpretive model valid for all the players in the game of the market. By electing "the" convention, the multitude *makes itself into a community*, almost as the election of a sovereign transforms the multitude into a people (we need not recall here that this process of abstraction is also and always concretely violent; on the concept of the multitude in post-Fordism, see Zanini and Fadini, 2001).

In a strongly linguistic economic system, therefore, the crisis of a convention means the explosion of the *body* of the multitude, of the plurality of the individual differences which, once again, must face the, if you will, historical task of producing/electing a new convention. Not an easy task, given that the global financial crisis is also a crisis of the multitude as "natural antecedent," its being by now a *historical result*, or better a global result, no longer reducible to a minority or to a "simple" enemy.

The Salient Features of Post-Fordism

Let's pick up the threads of what we've said so far. In order to understand the workings and the internal contradictions of the New Economy it is important to remember that it got its start with the frontal attack launched by the United States monetary authorities against the monetary effects of the Fordist paradigm (inflation and devaluation of the dollar on a worldwide scale). The Federal Reserve's monetarist initiative was aimed at reestablishing the state's power, leaving capital total freedom against its "enemies," both internal (the Fordist working class, rigidity of salaries and welfare programs) and external (impediments to US global expansion coming from "places" creating petrodollars and Eurodollars beyond control by the Fed). The idea was to tie the fate of American workers to the *risks* of American capital; to relaunch the *material* expansion of *American* capital in the world economy, eliminating all of the spaces in which the money created by the Federal Reserve was *no longer* transforming itself into capital, thus generating inflation (Reaganite neoliberalism should be interpreted above all, I believe, as a *nationalist ideology* within a world economy still structured along imperialistic lines). The diversion of savings to securities markets, initiated by the "silent revolution" in pension funds, has just this objective: to eliminate the separation between capital and labor implicit in the Fordist salary relationship by strictly tying workers' savings to processes of capitalist transformation/restructuring.

The stock exchange is precisely the mode of financing the economy which, contrary to bank financing (still prevalent in Europe, especially in the late 1970s), eliminates the wide-mesh spaces between savings and investments. With their savings invested in securities, workers are no longer separate from capital, as they are, by virtue of its legal definition, in the salary relationship. As shareholders they are tied to the ups and downs of the markets and so they are *co-interested* in the "good operation" of capital *in general*.

The financialization that came out of these historical conditions was the fruit of a precise, concrete, political initiative of the American capitalist state. It responded to the logic of the crisis-transformation of power relations between capital and wage labor and between nation-state and world economy. Any attempt to explain the crisis of the New Economy that does not take account of these historical precedents is bound to fail.

The silent revolution in pension funds, as we have seen, was in step with the crisis of the Fordist model centered not only on the centrality of the manufacturing sector and union mediation but, above all, on the *salary relationship*. The Fed's 1979 monetarist turn transformed salaries into an *adjustment variable* of the financial market. The overall income of workers and, through *stock options*, of management, was now tied to capitalist risk through the destandardization of salaries and the individualization of contract relationships.

In 1983, as a consequence of the Fed's monetarist turn, *competitive disinflation* started spreading through Europe, culminating, in 1986-87, in *financial deregulation*. Globalization, begun in the United States in the 1970s under the pressure of the struggle to detach incomes from the imperatives of social production, spread to the international level, forcing central banks to undertake the task of freeing themselves from the Keynesian policies of European governments. Competitive disinflation was the specific method with which structural imbalances in the public finances were attacked, forcing governments to renounce monetary financing of their own deficits and to look in turn to the financial markets. "If all that remains is the non-monetary option for financing deficits, then it is necessary to create the structures of a real financial market, capable of offering the savers who are invited to invest in government bonds the guarantee that they want most: reversibility. Only a vast, deep market, permanently animated by voluminous transactions offers players the certainty, at any moment, of finding a counterpart; that is, the possibility to get out without losing capital. This property has a name: liquidity" (Lordon, 2000, p. 23).

What followed from all this was the downgrading of the welfare state's role as a regulator of internal conflicts. The globalizing financial markets would bring about what we might call the *which-everness of nation-states*, the dependence of the financing of public spending on the dynamics of the global financial market and returns on securities. Again, (global) public opinion was played against the concrete, local individuality of the nation-states. The international monetary circuit, which up until the late 1970s rotated around the dollar as the national currency used in international transactions, had now been replaced by the international *financial* circuit rotating around *liquidity*, or the capacity to create credit-debt in response to public demand for investment.

The public demand for financing must be taken literally: it was no longer just the investment banks, or big business, or nation-states, but also wage-earners and salaried employees who wanted to participate as small investors in the big party organized by the securities markets. Financialization, which imposed itself on a global scale through competitive disinflation and the deregulation of capital markets, turned the public space into the place for the creation of liquidity, relegating to the back seat the payment of salaries through recourse to bank loans, the typical practice of the Fordist era, especially in European Rhineland capitalism unaccustomed to the impersonality of stock market financing.

The new configuration of global capitalism was driven by public opinion, the capacity to mobilize the *whicheverness*, the *mass* of investors, according to the logic of mimetic rationality. The Mexican crisis of 1994-95 and the Asian one in 1997, just like the Russian crisis of 1998, demonstrated the power of the reversibility of markets to effect the short-term movement of capital. They also featured the presence of institutional investors (pension funds and mutual funds) and the volume of the savings of western workers invested by them in emerging countries. Little did it matter, to the western worker-investor, if the security of his pension depended on reducing the Asian, Mexican, Russian, or Argentine proletariat to misery. Little did he care about the *content* of his own investments, or the fact that the decision to invest or disinvest had direct effects on the *bodies* of local populations.

We are not dealing here with indifference, or the desolidarization between citizens from rich countries and proletarians from poor countries. It is something much more profound, which has to do with the structural effects of information technologies and the revolution in business organization on the *nature* of work and on the relationship between work and worker. We must, therefore, examine the labor-production side of the New Economy, its most specifically post-Fordist aspect, in order to understand the nexus between the *whicheverness* of public opinion and individual forms of cognition, between the emerging financial convention and its social acceptance.

"Digital technologies," writes Franco Berardi, "open up a completely new perspective on work. First of all, they change the relationship between conception and execution, and therefore the relationship between the intellectual content of work and its material execution. Manual labor tends to be performed by machines commanded automatically, and innovative work, work which effectively produces value, is mental work. The material to be transformed is simulated by digital sequences. Productive work (work that produces value) consists in performing simulations which the computerized automatons then transfer onto the material" (Berardi, 2001, p. 50).

The individual's daily work at the computer is abstract while the knowledge content that the digital work allows to be produced is concrete and specific: "Digitalized work manipulates absolutely abstract signs, but its recombinant operations are highly specific, highly personalized, and therefore less and less interchangeable. Consequently, high-tech workers tend to consider their work the most essential part of their lives, the most singular and personalized. Exactly the contrary of the factory worker, for whom the eight hours of wage-labor were a kind of temporary death from which he awoke only when the siren sounded the end of the shift" (*ibid,*. p. 52).

Berardi's observations are a good starting point. What we would like to understand, in fact, is how the post-Fordist transformations of labor, in combination with processes of financialization, could give rise to that "financial convention," to that *patrimonial individualism* which shaped the New Economy, leading it to its takeoff and then to its crisis. The most attentive studies of transformations in the work place have brought to light the following aspects:

1) The post-Fordist mode of production came out of the *metabolizing of the social and cultural critique* of the Fordist model in the 1970s. It was able to do this because it put to work the most common, most public ("informal") qualities of the workforce—or better, language, communicative-relational action. This is the shared result of the toyotist revolution, of the widespread application of information technologies ("linguistic machines"), and of processes of externalization (*outsourcing*) (see, Chiapello and Boltanski, 1999; Fiocco, 1998).

2) Contrary to theories of the end of work, which actually were about the end of Fordist-Taylorist work, post-Fordism brought on a sizable increase in work time and an equally substantial reduction of wages and salaries. "The issue is not the end of work. The issue is work without end." (Cohen, 2001). The increase in the amount of work was the consequence of adding new blocks of social time to the time for strictly executive work: relational-communication

time, time for reflection, learning time (see Zarifan, 1995, 1996, 2001). Post-Fordism was structured so as to overcome the Tayloristic separation, sanctioned by the employment contract, of work and worker, between the work performed and the body of the worker. "Competence," "adaptability," "reactivity," "potential," became the criteria for recruitment of the workforce, especially of young workers.

3) With the explosion of the Fordist factory came the development of the reticular communicative space of the "virtual enterprise." Working in networks problematizes the collective perception of the individual dimension of exploitation. The atomization of work, its internal hierarchy, immigration, temp workers, *working poor*, are the social and identity vectors "played" against the class recomposition of the multiplicity of productive vectors. "Nevertheless," writes Marco Revelli, "this did not put an end to the capacity for centralization and subjugation (for private appropriation) of the disseminated forces of production by some higher-up on the 'chain of value': of the social power that governs the new disseminated productive system. It simply operates now in a less directly visible and material form (it too, like almost all powers nowadays, is an *invisible power*). It reinforces itself and subjugates by way of communicative and linguistic means (more than by personal chains of command or mechanical instruments), by activating symbolic and normative circuits (more than by physically delimiting technical spaces)" (Revelli, 2001). The concreteness of the exercise of symbolic power, for example through *branding policies*, has been well illustrated by Naomi Klein (2001); the separation of the brand from the production of the product and the vampirization of social criticism and grassroots trends on the part of large *corporations* in order to publicize and sell their products are

the globalized face of the post-Fordist transformation of work. More generally, economic power, insofar as it originates from the privatization of public resources (*common-use* resources, such as water and air, but also the lexicon of natural language) relies both on intellectual property rights (patents, *copyrights*) (Rifkin, 2000), and on forms of personal dependence: "Putting to work what is commonly shared," writes Paolo Virno, "that is to say, intellect and language, while on the one hand it renders fictitious the impersonal technical division of tasks, on the other hand, it induces a viscous personalization of subjugation. The unavoidable relationship with the presence of others, implied in the sharing of intellect, is seen as the universal restoration of personal dependence" (Virno, 2001).

4) The centrality of language in post-Fordist production and the putting to work of the cognitive properties of the workforce leads to the *crisis of measurability* of single work operations (of the work time necessary to produce goods). "When you can no longer define a performance norm *a priori*," writes Pierre Veltz, "there remains just one possibility: assigning objectives to work units and judging them *a posteriori*. When the analytical effort of elaborating detailed work procedures and transmitting them throughout highly hierarchical organizations becomes too costly, or useless, or impossible—or all three of these things—there remains the possibility of instituting a fabric of hierarchical rules into which will be inserted contractual relationships, to be updated from time to time, between the actors" (Veltz, 2000). The crisis of the measurability of value will reveal itself to be highly problematic in the late 1990s with the explosion of internet enterprises (the so-called Dot Coms).

5) The pervasiveness or absolutizing of the economic in the flexible post-Fordist society is a reflection of the pervasiveness of

language in the new mode of producing and selling of goods. We could speak of *semio-capital*, the semioticization of the social relations of production. The private has become public, and the public has become economic. As Federico Chicchi has written, "What allows us to link more general sociological reflections on the crisis of modernity to more specific ones having to do with the risk of social exclusion can be traced to the growing hegemony of the 'culture of risk' in the social context; a context which seems increasingly describable as an uncertain and fluid space, pervaded by the crisis of the institutions whose role in modernity was to connect the private sphere of life to the public" (Chicchi, 2001).

6) The post-Fordist revolution has in a certain sense gone beyond the *general intellect* described by Marx in the *Grundrisse*; that is to say, the technical-scientific knowledge accumulated in machines, in *fixed capital*, which makes work-time the "measurable basis" of value. In post-Fordism the *general intellect* is not fixed in machines, but in the *bodies* of workers. The body has become, if you will, the tool box of mental work. As Paolo Virno writes, "Marx identified the *general intellect* (or knowledge as the main productive force) with fixed capital, with the 'objective scientific capacity' in the system of machines, with no residuals. In so doing, he neglected the aspect in which the *general intellect* presents itself as living labor. We are obliged to raise this criticism by the analysis of post-Fordist production. In the so-called 'second generation of self-employment,' but also in a radically innovative factory like the Fiat plant in Melfi, it is not hard to recognize that the connection between knowledge and production is not at all limited to the system of machines, but is articulated in the linguistic cooperation of men and women, in their concrete concerted action. In the post-Fordist sphere a decisive role is played by conceptual constellations

and logical schemes which can never be condensed into fixed capital, since they are in fact inseparable from the interaction of a plurality of living subjects" (Virno, 2001).

We have synthesized some (only some, but the salient ones) of the characteristic features of the post-Fordist paradigm, those features which, in combination with processes of financialization, have given rise to the New Economy as a socially and culturally significant convention. It must be observed that transformations in the mode of production have had extremely important *deflationary effects*. In fact, the individualization and the insecuritization of work, as well as the externalization (*outsourcing*) of important segments of productive processes, have struck directly at the cost of labor, both in terms of salary and social costs (social security, pensions). This is an aspect which usually tends to be undervalued but which has played a very important role in provoking *banking disintermediation* in the relationship between savings and investments. In fact, because of deflation and the consequent decline in bank interest rates, savings have been attracted to securities markets throughout the world, and especially to markets in the U.S. Investment has thus been transferred from Treasury bonds to stocks by virtue of the structural transformations in the way of producing wealth.

Deflation is, we might say, the *monetary nexus* between post-Fordism and the New Economy. Pressure from pension funds and mutual funds has given rise to a "bullish convention" on exchange-listed equities, centered on value creation, which demands from enterprises a financial return detached from fundamental performance data. To satisfy the demands of Wall Street, businesses have developed restructuring plans (*downsizing*) and share reacquisition programs (*buybacks*) on such a massive scale that in the last few years net issuance of shares has even gone below zero. Combined with the strong demand from institutional funds, these programs provoke an increase in the imbalance between the supply and demand for shares which artificially (or inertially) pushes up the share price. A process that can be sustained as long as there is growth in the profits of companies listed on the stock exchange, but much less so, as has been the case since 1997, when profits start to trend downward. In which case, recourse to bank loans to take advantage of low interest rates and raise returns on equity only serves to further weaken a process that is in and of itself complex and vulnerable.

There is no doubt that the *cultural* determinants of the New Economy were the new technologies and what we call *general intellect* entrepreneurship. The success of *high-tech* stocks, and their collapse, can be explained in light of the attractive power of the new technologies over the collective imagination. The new technologies bring together, for better and for worse, phenomena attributable to the "new culture" of California and the restructuring of modes of production and work. The point of intersection is, not coincidentally, communication, language, the capacity of these "linguistic machines" to weave absolutely unprecedented webs of horizontal communication. "The webs which were," Revelli writes, reconstructing the sociocultural origins of the computer revolution, "the strongholds which condensed and gave shape in an informal way to a new figure of the century which conserved just one feature of the old-style producer—the capacity and the desire to 'mobilize technology' to transform the world—but which, contrary to the old producer, believed strongly in the value of decentralization, voluntary sharing, solidarity among peers, and free thought. At least as long as the double auroral phase lasted. Then came the third. The so-called *Cash Cow* phase" (Revelli, 2001, p. 110).

"Nobody," writes Po Bronson in his book on Silicon Valley, "can look at a nudist sitting there in his cubicle and see just dollar signs. Being a nudist on the late shift seemed to me to be the ultimate symbol of how people here want to assert their personal values on the job, a symbol of how tightly woven together work and play have become (a heck of a lot better symbol than a dentist trailer or an on-site washing machine). What some people see as a cold techno-Valley of ruthless corporate greed was nevertheless, to him, his Garden of Eden. And there was something innocent about nakedness, exposed and vulnerable. No money in the picture, no Ferraris, no lava lamps, no pocket protectors, no T-shirts, no distractions. Just a man, a computer, and a job" (Bronson, 2001, p.22).

The new technologies and the internet companies are the symbols of the expansion and the crisis of the New Economy because they summarize the salient features of the post-Fordist transformation (naked life, work, and vulnerability). The *high-tech* sector became a driving force at a moment when the flow of savings and capital (*venture capital*) onto the financial markets created, in what we might call a universal way, the New Economy as a dominant "convention." The multiplicity of individual beliefs "elected" the New Economy as an interpretative model of facts, choices, decisions, because the fusion between new technologies and financialization represented, for better or worse, the lived experience of millions of people coming to grips with the new post-Fordist paradigm.

The PC and internet companies became *cash cows*, money machines, when the stock exchanges succeeded in capitalizing the individualization of work, job insecurity, risk, desire for liberation of/from work, counter culture, the desire to change the world. In order to make the New Economy a convention, as Keynes defined it, risk capital had to be freed from the processes of disinflation and banking disintermediation.

But also necessary was a *technological paradigm* capable of influencing the choices of investors, of "pulling" the markets, of forcing them in one direction rather than another, of fusing the essence of the new work and public opinion. If, as Virno says, "the communication (or 'culture') industry plays a role analogous to that played traditionally by the *industry of the means of production*: if it is, that is, a special productive sector, which, however, determines the instruments and the procedures which will then be largely applied in every angle of the social productive process" (Virno, 2001); or if, as Po Bronson says, "Middle Americans missed their chance to buy Data General in 1975 and Microsoft in 1986, so when they hear there's a whole 'nother computer revolution going on, they don't want to buy the software so much as they want to buy the stock of the company that makes the software. But that's fine with the people out here. They'll be happy to take your money" (Bronson, 2001, p.32); then the New Economy *as convention* is language itself, *language as means of production and circulation of goods*.

Critical Observations on Work Time

The best approach to understanding the transformations and collapse of the Fordist model is to analyze its rearticulation of the relationship between capital and labor. There have been multiple and wide-ranging changes that go from the streamlining and increased flexibility of productive processes to the externalizing of entire segments of the workforce (subcontracting, *outsourcing*);

from the delocalizing of production around the globe to the generalized application of communicative technologies (virtualization); from the enhanced evaluation of the local territory as a complex social resource (industrial districts) to financial globalization. In other words, analysis of the crisis-transformation of the Fordist model must not focus on the progressive reduction of blue collar workers and the dwindling presence of large factories, but rather on the outright redefinition of the *nature* of work. The nature of work has been changing in at least two directions which, I believe, are fundamental: its increasing autonomization, in the form of the growing strategic importance of neo-self-employment; and its communicative-relational, we might say *linguistic*, character. More and more, work means communicating and increasingly the relationship between capital and labor has been de-salaryized (the *dejobbing* phenomenon), and this brings with it a radical change in the way conflicts are joined.

These changes in ways of working, changes that mark the end of Fordism and the beginning of post-Fordism or the New Economy, are only partially related to what has been defined, often improperly, as market globalization, the entrance of a growing number of emerging countries into the international division of labor and trade. The increased competitiveness in world markets and an overall decline in purchasing power of wages and salaries have, paradoxically, compressed, constricted, and limited market outlets. Today, producing means exploiting every minimal oscillation in demand; it means "breathing with the market," bringing it, if you will, inside the factory. Producing means *responding* to demand, not making it depend on the supply of goods, as used to be the case in the Fordist economy. This reversal of the relationship between demand and supply is at the origins of the entry of communication directly into the productive process, in the sense that the chain of production has, in fact, become a *linguistic chain*, a *semantic connection*, in which communication, the transmission of information, has become both a raw material and an instrument of work, just like electricity. Communication and language make possible what in the Fordist model was an obstacle, that is to say, the articulation of mechanization and flexibility. As Enzo Rullani has written, "you can mechanize without losing flexibility; you can organize flexible response systems not by investing directly in machinery and *firm specific* knowledge, but, for example, by making use of *outsourcing* networks" (Rullani, 1998). Moreover, it is technologized communication that makes it possible to speak of the New Economy as "reticular capitalism," a capitalism in which semantic investments, the linguistic sharing of diffuse knowledge, foster the new international division of labor, of labor which is increasingly *cognitive*.

Another fundamental feature of the Fordist model has also gone by the wayside: the separation between work and worker so typical of the scientific model of Frederick Winslow Taylor. Today the capitalist organization of work aims to overcome this separation, to *fuse* work and worker, to *put to work the entire lives* of workers. Skills, rather than professional qualifications, are put to work and with them workers' emotions, feelings, their after-work lives, we might say the whole life of the *linguistic community*. Thanks to new technologies and to the reticular organization of productive/distributive processes, knowledge is no longer embodied in "some other thing," in machines or materials or finished products, but in *knowledge work* itself. Communication support systems—codes, languages, shared meanings—allow knowledge to circulate on its own, independently of fixed capital and legal ownership. Basically for this reason, the concept of productivity no longer has anything to do with Fordist productivity (the famous economies of scale, for which the reduction of unit cost was obtained by increasing the quantity of the product). Today's productivity is increasingly determined by the capacity to respond to unforeseen and unforeseeable situations, *emergent situations*, those situations which make any sort of planning impracticable, assigning a central role to *occasionality*. But this productivity would be unthinkable without the dematerialization of support systems and means of transmitting knowledge, without the constant mentalization of capital, its fusion with living labor. *The reproducibility*, at low cost and in less and less time, of knowledge not embodied in fixed machines is another factor at the origin of *increasing returns*, of the possibility to unshackle productivity from scarce resources, such as labor and constant capital in the Fordist-industrial economy. In the post-Fordist paradigm, the limit, the necessary cost of production, becomes *the life itself of the linguistic community*.

It is possible that this new nature of work, its being *active life* more than work separated from the biological-reproductive sphere, could lead to the end of the *category* of work. This analytical hypothesis, moreover, is the underlying basis for work reduction/redistribution models aimed at combating unemployment. It is a controversial issue which must be examined at some length.

It is certainly true that, over the long run, the average life-time dedicated to *salaried* work has decreased substantially; over the span of the last century it decreased by half. And it is equally true that, parallel to the reduction in salaried work time, we have witnessed the crisis of industrial time as homogenous, abstract, chronometric, computable objectifiable time, external to human beings and to things; a crisis, one might say, of Newtonian time. We must, however, be careful not to draw hasty conclusions from this overall reduction in salaried work time. I disagree completely, for example, with those who, *on this basis*, have elaborated an *ideology of free time* in the name of which they propose to reduce work time in order to better distribute it, aiming in this way to combat unemployment.

When we analyze the relationship between work and life, production and reproduction and "free time," in reality we are analyzing the relationship between, and the internal articulation of, *blocks of social time*. We are analyzing, that is, the *structuring relationship* between productive work time, domestic work time, and free time. The ideology of free time arises from a statistical calculation according to which an average day's contractual work time, divided among the total over-15 population, comes out to approximately 2 1/2 hours. From which it follows that, since time freed from work amounts to about 70% of our waking time, "free time" is the dominant element in the structure of social time blocks. In other words, today we work an average of 2 1/2 hours a day!

Through the invention of the fictitious average day of the fictitious average person, mixing together men and women, all age groups over 15, and even working people and nonworking people, this way of calculating the size of the various blocks of social time denies the heterogeneity of populations. It denies the social and personal importance of biographical rhythms, as though time had the same weight in the concrete lives of all individuals and was not experienced in subjectively different ways, as though someone working 8 hours in their active life were fictitiously living in their retirement. This way of reasoning naively considers domestic work time as free time and denies the structuring nature of professional time and domestic time on what remains of waking time on an average day.

It is important to emphasize these methodological questions because, if the sociological analysis of time in the *Fordist* era is permeated by such ingenuous oversimplifications, imagine what and how much confusion we'll be deluged with in the post-Fordist era, deriving from the misunderstanding of the temporal dimension of the average social life! In reality, in the last twenty years the average social working day has become *longer* rather than shorter. A very rigorous and significant study of this phenomenon has been conducted by the American sociologist Juliet Schor. In *The Overworked American*, Schor demonstrates that over the course of the twenty years leading up to the early 1990s, the average American workday (professional and domestic) had actually lengthened, to the point where Americans were left with only 16 1/2 hours of free time per week. ("If the trends continue," Schor writes on page one, "by the end of the century Americans will be spending as much time at their job as they did back in the nineteen twenties.") So much for the "centrality of leisure time!" If this quantitative increase in the time dedicated to professional and domestic work is then analyzed in light of the new characteristics of productive time resulting form the post-Fordist transformation of work, it becomes evident that the question of time and the reduction of professional time is quite complex and in no way resolvable in purely contractual terms.

The only point on which there exists what we might call a general consensus is the reduction of work time *immediately necessary* to material production, which is to say the reduction of time dedicated to the *execution* of manual actions in the production of objects. This is the effect of automation which, it should be recalled, is not a new technology but a very old concept of technics. Although it is true that automation has brought about a significant contraction of the time and fatigue of executory manual labor, and although it is true that automation can free up more available time for other activities, it is nevertheless equally true that *the work time immediately necessary for material production is no longer the essential element of productive activity in the broad sense.* Alongside the reduction of "classical" Newtonian-Taylorist time, on which the control of wage and salary costs still concentrate, we have seen the emergence of *new times*: time dedicated to dealing with production events/emergencies, time involved in the design of projects for innovation, training time, time for relating, such as making and maintaining contacts with suppliers and customers, contracting time between services or occupations, time for listening to and talking with consumers-users.

A closer look shows that while on the one hand there has been a reduction in machine-commanded time *separate* from the worker's body, on the other hand there has been an explosive increase in the linguistic-communicative-relational time of living labor, the time that in the New Economy involves inter-subjective communication or value-creating cooperation.

The linguistic nature of social work time in the post-Fordist regime partially undercuts the analysis of the post-Fordist paradigm from the point of view of the system of enterprises, while at the same time it forces us to redefine social productivity *starting from* the social territory. It is the social territory (the industrial district, the region, the nation, or the set of countries) that defines the limits of growth and productivity; it is the territory as *concrete community*, over which to exercise capitalistic *command*, which has been the target of restructuring and reorganization of the international division of cognitive work.

But to return to the question of reducing work hours to create new jobs, it is important to understand that one of the most perverse effects of the ideology of free time has been to confuse the terms of the political struggle on the terrain of the new social relationships of production. The misunderstanding of the linguistic nature of post-Fordist work, arising from a vision of production time as Newtonian-Taylorist time commanded by the knowledge embodied in fixed capital, in machines separate from living labor, has caused more than a few people to believe in the possibility of combating unemployment by reducing exactly that work time immediately necessary to production which counts less and less from the point of view of capital productivity. This amounts to trying to resolve an economic contradiction economically; which means trying to create employment by denying the productive power of living labor, which means redistributing the *poorest* kind of work in the name of *Fordist* full occupation.

The only way to force capital to create employment in order to reabsorb "excess" workers is by *freeing up blocks of living time*, by reducing, for example, the work week by a day. This by way of saying, moreover, that if we believe it is right to fight for the reduction of work time it is because reducing work time is above all an objective tied to the *quality of life*, and not to the need to create new jobs. The reduction of work hours is a *project* for the future; it is *not* the current state of affairs.

The ethical dimension, if you will, of the reduction of working hours shows itself in the struggle to improve the quality of life, not in the desire to free up jobs. And the same goes, furthermore, for the history of the labor movement's fight to reduce working hours, from Marx onwards. It is useful to recall, for those who are still prisoners of the "Volkswagon syndrome," that the reason for that famous agreement between the union and top management had nothing to do with any political concept of citizenship but, much more prosaically, with flexibilizing the work force in order to adjust the payroll to the volume of orders; all in order to save $254 on each car produced. The agreement's primary objective, in other words, was *economic* and not the "ethical-political" one of creating new jobs. So much so, in fact, that the agreement did not translate into new hiring but into non-firings. Nobody denies that, on the union's part, there was a sense of solidarity in trying to avoid a wave of layoffs in the automobile industry, at the cost of cutting salaries. But the fact remains that the appeal to solidarity came in response to an initiative by VW management whose objective was to redefine company earnings by lowering labor costs.

The French *reduction du temps de travail* (RTT)—the 35 hour week (or better, the 1600 hour year) introduced by Jospin in 1998 and affecting for the moment 15.1 million workers (65% percent of businesses employing more than 20 workers) has "liberated" from 11 to 16 vacation days per year, but it has also meant, for the 63% of workers surveyed by the French research institute Dares, a substantial increase in productivity and stress. The free (or liberated) days have been chosen primarily by employers (for example, always Monday or always Friday) so that flexibility has been accomplished unilaterally. In fact, the reduction in work hours has allowed employers (confederated in the Medef) to increase productivity and to freeze or reduce salaries and wages. For 85% of the work force, salaries have actually declined. Finally, the increase in pension and health care costs induced by the RTT have been more than compensated for by government subsidies to business. It is estimated that the RTT has created a sixth of all new jobs, not very many if you take into account the disproportionate increase in productivity compared to the reduction in work time.

"Most factory workers have experienced it (the RTT and the incorporation into their effective work time of break time and Saturdays) as a regression, and CGT (union) activists see it as a hidden way of taking back rights won by the struggles of 'older generations' ... So the workers are supposed to resign themselves to considering the question of their material well-being as an accessory, as though they should give up trying to obtain an improvement of their income. It seems as though, in the name of the redistribution of employment, they have been condemned to being kept floating just above the surface, under the permanent threat of sinking down among the working poor and the RMIsts [welfare recipients]" (Beaud and Pialoux, 2000, p. 423).

To sum up, people are working more and more, *and that in itself should be enough to create new jobs*, without reducing contractual work time and without (in all probability) reducing salaries. It is difficult, in fact, in the presence of a significant reduction in the duration of work, to avoid an increase in salary costs and no business, in a particularly intense competitive environment, will agree to assume this risk and see its competitiveness threatened. For this reason, in most cases the reduction in work time has also been accompanied by a (though less than proportionate) reduction in salary or, as in France, by the *annualization* of the flexible work schedule. The question of combating unemployment involves above all the *creation-distribution of new incomes*, and not the reduction of existing income consequent to its redistribution between the employed and the unemployed.

On the linguistic dimension of money

Another question worth examining is the global and financial dimension of post-Fordism. I partially agree with those who submit that, with respect to processes of internationalization in the last century, today's globalization is nothing particularly new. It seems to me, however, that there is an important aspect of today's global-ization that allows us to speak of unprecedented processes destined to last a long time. In particular, I'm thinking of the *financializa-tion of household economies*, the diversion of an increasingly larger part of family savings to securities markets around the world in the hopeful search for increasing returns.

This constitutes a break in the Fordist circuit of savings which placed *national* Treasury Notes at the center of families' deferred income (or complementary or supplemental income if we think of pension funds). The consequences of this new trend are hard to predict. To be sure, we are witnessing a globalization or worldwide distribution of *risk*, an unprecedented "social construction of risk," which must be read together with the downsizing of the national welfare state. The national "community of risk" thus seems to be going by the wayside while the global State, the supra-national State, is taking on decisive importance. If we add the fact that this financialization of savings has its origins in the *deflationary character* of the post-Fordist mode of production, in the fact, that is, that pension funds find themselves having to pay out benefits that will have appreciated over time, and therefore must look for elevated and thus risky returns, we can understand that the *direct* origins of the new financial globalization lie in structural changes in modes of production.

One of the biggest difficulties in analyzing the last twenty years of transformations in finance capital and its role in the crisis of liberalist globalization regards precisely our understanding of *dis-inflation* as a long-term structural process. The difficulty is partly theoretical, given that in the history of capitalism long-term growth trends have been largely of an inflationary nature, so that theoretical research (and particularly Marxist research) has been concentrated above all on the *opposition* between money and credit. But the difficulty is also political, because disinflation interacts directly with the financialization of household economies, with the increase of financial holdings in the structure of family savings and, consequently, with the increasingly important role of institutional investors in the dynamics of the global financial system.

The difficulty is political because the financialization of spheres of life, aside from being a reflection of some significant demographic modifications and an indication of a historic turning point in the redistributive role of the welfare state, forces us to go beyond the Hilferdinghian and monetarist *dichotomy* between a (increasingly less defined) "real economy" and a "financial market" which seems to many of us to have taken on a life of its own. "Neither of the two major interpretations," writes Lorenzo Cillario, "is convincing on this point; neither the 'bourgeois' theory, close to neoclassical and monetarist philosophies, nor the interpretation of a certain 'critical' thought, which misunderstands the Marxian matrix from which it presumes to derive. The first theorizes an autonomy of monetary and financial courses, attributing it to the extreme idea that money enjoys a life of its own; that capital is self-generating and has nothing to do with human work and the process of production; imagining that wealth is created or destroyed by intrinsic virtues and vices. The other accuses the financial market of expressing only speculative and fictitious characteristics; the upward movements of the indexes and the stock markets are only 'speculative bubbles' while declines, in all likelihod, are the just punishment that financial activity must undergo for its perverse inclination, inscribed in its very nature, to distort the behavior of the real economy" (Cillario, 1998).

A historical reconstruction of financial globalization over the last twenty years, as we have seen, allows us to characterize disinflation (the progressive reduction of the rate of inflation) as a structural process initiated *before* the Asian crisis, before, that is, the crisis that is generally considered as the primary cause of the drop in prices in internationally traded goods. This fact is extremely important, in the first place because it locates the beginning of the disinflationary process at the apex of the international economy, namely in the United States, with Volker's monetarist reversal in October 1979. In the second place, the disinfationary process finds its overall transformative strength in the contradiction between the tradition of monetary language and the innovation of capital enhancement processes. It is the *resistance* of the traditional Fordist-inflationist languages (both workers' resistance and the resistance of Keynesian rationality: the top-down rigidity of the salary variable) in the face of the attack by capital against the working class that is at the origin of one of the most spectacular leaps forward in technology and processes of financialization in the history of capitalism. The flexibilizing of productive processes and the externalizing of the social costs of labor which have brought about the growth of second generation self-employment are the results of the tension between the desire to destroy the social composition of Fordism and the "rational expectations implicit in anti-inflationary monetarist policy" (see Marazzi, 1998). Thirdly, the disgregation of the Fordist socio-economic configuration brought about the transition to the economy of *increasing returns*. The putting to work of the language of social relations, the activation of productive cooperation beyond the factory gate, is the origin of the economy of increasing returns which responds to declining profit rates by intensifying the exploitation of the communicative-relational cooperation of the workforce.

As stated earlier, "increasing returns" means that it is no longer constant physical (fixed) capital, nor even employment levels that determine the productivity thresholds of living labor. Returns increase because constant capital itself has become linguistic (the body of the entire society has become, so to speak, "constant capital"). The *powerful effectiveness* of the agents of capital has been transposed, directly internalized in the social workforce.

For some time now in the United States *capital expenditures* by companies listed on the stock exchange are 98% financed within the companies themselves, so that dividends, interest, mergers and acquisitions (M&A) and buybacks, or rather the sum total of the financial income transferred by the companies to their shareholders, is produced with money borrowed from the banking system and used for operations on the securities markets (those very operations which generate financial income). From 1985 to 1997, the total of dividends, interest, M&A and *buybacks* came to some 5% more than the total for capital investments (see Henwood, 1998).

In other words, debt owed to banks by companies serves to finance not capital investments but rather a sort of Keynesian *effective demand*, even more so when a part of the financial wealth available to the mass of household economies derives from investments in securities. In 1998, for example, the liquid assets of American families amounted to 13,800 billion dollars, of which 43% was held in stocks, 23% in bank deposits, and 17% in mutual funds. And where savings are lacking, private debt is what maintains the elevated levels of aggregate consumer demand. This is a trend in progress not only in the United States but in all economically developed countries.

"Certainly, "writes Orléan, "shares are not money. Their liquidity is only partial in the sense that they are not accepted as universal instruments of exchange. Nevertheless, their sphere of circulation is already extremely vast, not only as reserve assets, but also as means of exchange for certain types of transactions. We see this when one company acquires another with the help of its own shares, or even better when a manager accepts to be paid in stock options. For this reason, then, we can consider shares as constituting an embryonic form of currency even if they still can't be used to purchase consumer goods. The question of whether or not this form will arrive at maturity, whether it will become a currency in the full sense of the term, is in a certain sense the challenge of our analysis because such a turn of events would constitute a radical change in the principle of sovereignty." (Orléan, 1999, p. 242)

We have arrived at an important point in our analysis of the nature of the New Economy. We have seen how financialization is centered on the concept of liquidity. We have likewise observed that liquidity is a function (or, Marxistly speaking, a natural form) of money which embodies the action of public opinion on the multiplicity of subjects participating in the economy of the financial markets. To function as a lever of the choices/decisions of investors, public opinion must equip itself with a convention or an interpretive model considered by everyone as "true," or *dominant*. This convention is produced by society itself, and historically it is expressed in the complex form of the social relationships of production, consumption, and imagination. In the New Economy the convention (social *and* financial) has been expressed as a technological linguistic-communicative paradigm.

The phenomenal growth of financial liquidity, which has led some to define the New Economy superficially as "casino capitalism," actually signals a *displacement* of monetary creation from the central bank to the financial markets. Indeed, public opinion, its communicative action, originated the quantity of liquidity that the central bank maintained over the course of the 1990s. The supply of money grew, certainly in the United States but not only there, *independently* of any quantitative objective (pre) determined by the central monetary authorities. Instead, it grew in response to the increase in demand from investors, both companies and private citizens. The Federal Reserve did nothing other than *monetize* this demand for liquidity generated by the action of public opinion.

From the perspective of a *qualitative* analysis of the form of money—as we shall see later—the displacement of monetary creation from the sphere of the central bank to the financial markets *brings about a change in the nature of sovereignty.* (Note that this does not mean that the financial markets create their own specific currency, distinct from that created by the central bank; it means that the central bank, in order to perform its role as the creator of money in the last instance to assure the circulation of liquid assets, is forced to follow the movements of the financial markets).

Where the creation of liquidity is preeminently a *banking* function, sovereignty belongs to the national State. Where, on the other hand, the creation of liquidity is preeminently *financial*, sovereignty belongs to public opinion and the sociofinancial convention which is historically proper to it. In the first case, the form of money defines a way of belonging to society based on the principle of *citizenship*. In the second case, the case of financial liquidity, the form of money defines a sense of belonging that is supranational, a *global* citizenship in which the regime of opinion prevails over the representative regime of the nationally constituted State.

The New Economy and Attention Deficit

Before analyzing in detail the dynamics of the business cycle and the crisis of the New Economy (see Part II), it may do well to take a brief look at one of the bigger contradictions generated, on the one hand, by the increase in knowledge/reflective work time typical of post-Fordism and, on the other, by the limitless expansion of the so-called infosphere. In his book, *La fabbrica dell'infelicità* (*The Unhappiness Factory*), Berardi has written, "The technological context is marked by the constant acceleration of the rhythms of the global machine, by the constant expansion of cyberspace with respect to the limited capacity of the individual brain, with respect to cybertime. The communicational context is one of limitless expansion of the infosphere, that is, of the sphere that contains the signals on which competitiveness depends, on which survival depends. Aren't we dealing with a situation very similar to that suggested by the Greek etymology of the term panic?" (Berardi, 2001, p.78). The Greek root of panic is *pan*, meaning "all that exists," and the divinity identified with the name expresses himself as the carrier of a "sublime madness" which disturbs those who are visited by him.

Thomas Davenport and John Beck have examined this conflict between cyberspace and cybertime in their *The Attention Economy: Understanding the New Currency of Business* (2001). In the New Economy "what is scarce is human attention. The width of the telecommunications band is not a problem, the problem is the width of the human band." According to the authors, the technological revolution has certainly enlarged social access to information enormously, but the limitless growth in the supply of information conflicts with a *limited* human demand, which is all the more limited the more work time reduces the attention time we are able to dedicate to ourselves and to the people with whom we work and live.

We are, that is, in a situation of *information glut*, of an excess, an overload, of information. The Sunday edition of the *New York Times* contains more information than all of the written material available to readers in the 15th century. "Back then the problem was not finding the time to read, but finding enough reading material to fill up the time. Information was a sellers' market, and books were thought to be more precious than, say, peasants."

To take another example of the *information glut*—beyond those regarding the number of books published every year (300 thousand in the world) or the exponential growth of information available on the internet (2 billion web pages in the world, with the volume of web traffic doubling every 100 days), to the multiplication of data banks (there are now 11,339 databases on the market)—today an average size supermarket carries something like 40,000 different items. Faced with the obvious impossibility of attracting the attention of the average consumer to the total supply of goods, his attention is literally purchased. In 1999 producers of nondurable goods in the United States spent 25 billion dollars on marketing, which is to say *five times* the profits earned by supermarket chains in the same year!

Another example: if the world's entire population (6 billion people) were to speak continuously for a whole year, all of the words pronounced could be transmitted in just a few hours by the potential capacity of telecommunications systems produced between 1996 and 2000.

The imbalance between the supply and demand for attention lies at the root of the panic-depressive syndrome called *infostress*, to the point that sales of the drug Ritalin used in the treatment of

Attention Deficit Disorder (ADD) have increased 9 times from 1990 to today (see Gilioli and Gilioli, 2001).

The *attention economy* is the product of the high rate of growth of access to information provoked by new technologies, in that in order to maintain or simply attract customers/consumers it is necessary to capture their attention. And this costs more and more all the time. It is a cost that increases as the unit cost of production decreases. The New Economy is in fact characterized on the supply side by the law of *increasing returns*, a law which has managed to impose itself after the law of diminishing returns went by the wayside with the diminished importance of raw materials relative to intangible resources. But the fact is that, on the *demand* side for goods and services, attention (and its allocation) has *diminishing* returns, it has, that is, taken the place of the physical raw materials of the industrial economy. It is a *scarce* and extremely *perishable good* (if attention goes in one direction it cannot simultaneously go in another, and if too much attention is required to perform a certain task, every marginal unit of attention time will diminish). "What information consumes," Herbert Simon, Nobel prize winner for economics, has said, "is rather obvious: it consumes the attention of its targets. Hence a wealth of information creates a poverty of attention."

In the expansion phase of the New Economy, internet companies were strongly motivated in the pursuit of the attention of web users and for this reason they were financially rewarded by a steady flow of venture capital in search of elevated returns. The speculative bubble was in a certain sense inevitable, owing, not surprisingly, to the structural imbalance between the infosphere and the human capacity to consume the attention socially necessary to realize the overall supply of information.

On closer look, this is an outright paradox. On the one hand, the post-Fordist revolution has attempted to overcome the disaffection with Fordist-Taylorist work by bringing into play management techniques for the "transfer of autonomy" and the "personalization of work." What came out of all this was the *reflective work* described by, among others, Ulrich Beck. On the other hand, however, this transfer of autonomy and responsibility has not desaturated work at all, has not in the least alleviated its intensity or diminished its weight in the life of workers. On the contrary, it has added a heavier burden, a more absorbent integration into the system of the integrated and fully socialized factory. By putting to work even nonoccupational skills and resources, by eliminating *non-productive* time, the post-Fordist transformation of the world of work has reduced the quantity of attention time necessary to absorb the total supply of informational goods.

In this *crisis of disproportion* between attention supply and demand it is inevitable that competition leads to processes of *monopolization* of the production and distribution of information. But although monopoly can reduce the number of competitors on the supply side of informational goods, it cannot however overcome the structural divergence in attention supply and demand. In addition to being human, this divergence is also *monetary*: if in order to command attention it is necessary to invest more and more money (in addition to owning the intellectual property rights), in order to sell/realize the supply after eliminating the competition there must be on the demand side (or, if you will, on the side of the consumption of attention) sufficient income to acquire the informational goods offered on the market.

But this additional income doesn't seem to be available to everyone, or at least not to the majority of consumers. In the *attention economy*, income, rather than increasing, seems instead to diminish and it diminishes in relation to the increase in the quantity of time dedicated to work. If, on the other hand, attention time increases then the time dedicated to earning a salary inevitably decreases.

We will see how the crisis of the New Economy in the late 1990s can be explained on the basis of this disproportion between information supply and attention demand. What we have described, it is well to recall, is a capitalistic contradiction, a contradiction internal to the value form, to its being contemporaneously commodity and money, a commodity increasingly accompanied by information (necessary to carve out a market niche) and money-income increasingly distributed in a way that does not increase effective demand. The financialization of the 90s certainly generated additional incomes but, aside from distributing those additional incomes unequally, it created them by *destroying* salary and stable employment. The destruction of stable employment and regular wages and salaries contributed to aggravating the attention deficit of worker-consumers, forcing them to dedicate more attention to looking for work than to consuming goods and services. The conditions posed by financial markets for the creation of investment returns actually promoted the *downsizing, reengineering, outsourcing,* and *mergers and acquisitions* which brought unprecedented insecurity for the workforce. The capital necessary to the production of informational goods was in fact subtracted from the remuneration of the qualities of the workforce put to work in the post-Fordist factory. There was a failure to take into account that the workforce is not only a producer, but also a consumer of attention, not only salary cost, but also income.

2

The New Business Cycle

A Chronicle of the 2001 Financial Crisis

The need to take a hard look at the *business cycle* of the New Economy became apparent in October 2000 when the global markets came up against a *liquidity crunch* which until then had seemed unimaginable. An accumulation of critical factors—oil prices, the situation in the Middle-East, the steady decline of stock indexes starting in March of that same year, the evaporation of a host of Dot Com enterprises, the chain of financial failures throughout Asia, and the weakness of the Euro—combined to bring about a *risk reassessment* which created more than a few financial difficulties for the world economy. According to an initial analysis by *Business Week* conducted in the heat of the moment, it looked like there could be an increasing risk of recession over the course of 2001 because, unlike the Asian and Russian crises, the end-of-century liquidity crisis had hit both the financial markets and the banks at the same time.

Stephen Roach, an economist at Morgan Stanley, commented that the economy had entered "the first recession of the information age" which he described as a classic example of an unsustainable investment boom, adding that it would take some time to clean out the excess. The data reported by *Business Week* on the overproduction of goods and services in the U.S. economy (*Too Much of Everything*, 9 April 2001) were striking. In the telecommunications sector, only 2.5-3% of fiber-optic networks were actually being used to transmit data. In Taiwan, for example, makers of semi-conductors were working at 70% of productive capacity and in just the first six months of 2001 global spending on investments had diminished by 16%. The entire computer sector had been hit by a drop in demand and the number of lay-off announcements kept on rising. In the automobile sector, after years of building new plants just about everywhere, the slowdown in demand was leading to closures and layoffs; retail sales and advertising both saw drastic reductions.

This excess of production, according to Roach as well as Federal Reserve Chairman Alan Greenspan, had been caused by an increase in productivity which was *only apparent*. The increased productivity was to be attributed, that is, more to higher volumes of investment in *high tech* (more output at the same level of input) than to greater efficiency in business organization. Even when this was taken into account, the fact remained that starting in 1995 the average annual productivity growth had been 2.4%, double the rate from 1973 to 1990.

The question itself is controversial because, despite the slow-down in high-tech investments (from 31.4% at the start of 2000 to 10.7% in the first quarter of 2001), companies continued to invest. According to a study by Price Waterhouse Cooper, companies that had invested in new technologies saw productivity increases of 13.4% over the course of 2000 (in the last quarter of 2000, and thus after the slowdown had already begun, productivity still increased by 2.2%), while for those that hadn't invested in information technology, productivity increased by only 4.9% (see

Fortune, "Buried in Tech," 16 April 2001). In theory, therefore, the *buyers' strike* by companies might turn out to be only temporary.

Spending by American consumers, which during the first half of 2001, had not declined at all despite the high rate of household indebtedness, was in danger of collapse if unemployment continued to rise. And not a day went by without a few thousand more workers losing their jobs. Nevertheless, the first half of 2001 actually saw an *increase* in consumer spending of 2.5% in *real terms*. This paradox is explained by the increase in housing prices: more than 9% from June 2000 to June 2001, the greatest increase in ten years. While, on the one hand, the drop in stock prices had primarily affected high income families, who have a low propensity toward spending, and while, at the same time, the wealth effect (lower stock prices, lower consumer spending) would not be felt on a large scale until Americans took notice of the reduction of their pension benefits, then it is plausible that the wealth effect should be felt above all in the housing sector. Consumer spending, thanks to mortgage refinancing, was able to resist and continue to help contain the risk of recession. Underlying this phenomenon in fact, beyond the reduction in mortgage interest rates induced by the economic stimulus policies of the Federal Reserve, were important demographic factors, such as the increase in demand for housing caused by the rise in the number of single-person households.

According to Paul Krugman (2001) and even according to the IMF, Bush's tax cuts would not help at all, concentrated as they were among taxpayers at the highest income brackets (about 40% of the tax cuts went into the pockets of the top 1% on the income distribution scale) and in any event they came too late with respect to the fast-paced onset of the recession.

The Center-Periphery Model

Analysis of the *global effects* of the crisis of the American New Economy is essential if we wish to refine the only economic model still capable of telling us something about the genesis of the crisis and the transformation of the international monetary and financial system: the center-periphery model, once known as the developed-underdeveloped or North-South model. "Refine" it in the sense of making it less mechanistic, because the analysis of today's social processes of production and distribution of goods casts light on what the center-periphery model leaves in shadow, which is to say, on the *internal contradictions* of the dominant countries, the countries of the center (see De Cecco, 1998). We must, in other words, *defetishize* a model which, while having the merit of establishing the right balance between cause and effect in the functioning of the global financial system, runs the risk of representing the system in a circular, and politically impractical, conception.

The center-periphery model starts with the United States, the center country *par excellence*, which from the 1971 declaration of the dollar's nonconvertibility into gold and the subsequent establishment of the floating exchange rate system, has continued to affect monetary policy throughout the world. In this model, the center countries are the major creditors in so far as they have at their disposition an enormous quantity of savings which they decide to disburse, naturally with the aim of producing returns, on the basis of available information regarding the condition of their potential debtors. So a position of advantage will be occupied by those countries which, by reason of the culture and organization of the banking and financial system, are located closer to the center, while countries located on the periphery of the empire, and about which the available information is "imperfect" or hard to verify, will be at a disadvantage.

When credit terms in center countries are easier, generally when interest rates are low, the banks also make an effort to satisfy requests for loans from those countries which have most recently become part of the international financial community, countries for which information is less precise and more costly to obtain, and where future recovery of the loans will be more difficult. When instead credit terms in center countries are worse, because interest rates in the United States are higher, there is a wave of credit withdrawal, a backlash which penalizes above all but not only peripheral countries about which information is weak or insufficient. It should be noted that a determining factor in the model we have just described is the movement of interest rates in center countries.

In terms of the model, therefore, the offer of credit depends on the *internal* conditions of the major lending countries, that is, on the phases of their economic cycle. If, for example, the Federal Reserve lowers interest rates with the aim of stimulating the American economy or of heading off a financial crisis, the immediate effect is that international capital moves to Germany or Japan, leading to a rise in the exchange value of the mark (today the Euro) or the yen. Germany and Japan, in order to prevent their exports from becoming less competitive because of currency appreciation, then lower their interest rates, causing capital to flow toward Latin America or Asia.

This gives rise to a race for higher returns by banks and financial investors from the entire developed world, a race which can only be won by extending the borders of the area in which loans are made, to include, therefore, countries normally excluded from the club of debtor nations in times of restrictive monetary policy.

This dynamic has accelerated over the course of the last twenty years as a consequence of the free movement of capital. The acceleration began in the 1980s, within the United States, when the Reagan administration allowed the Savings & Loan Associations to make financial investments in addition to the traditional home loans, and then, starting in the early 1990s, on an international scale, when the International Monetary Fund (IMF) allowed institutional investors, which are the big collectors of private savings, to invest anywhere. The financialization of household savings, the diversion of assets managed by nonbanking institutions (pension funds and mutual funds) from the traditional and more secure treasury notes of national governments to stock exchanges around the world, continued gathering force as disinflation caused interest rates to decline, making banks less attractive for savings.

To avoid a crisis brought on by the shift of savings toward securities with higher rates of return, banks first turned to the real estate market, provoking a crisis by granting loans on absurd conditions, and then to securities markets. Banks thus became global concerns, disengaging from the local management of savings and giving priority to asset management and to improving their own share price for their shareholders (*shareholder value*).

The fact that in the center-periphery model credit terms and conditions are determined in the first place by the center countries became a point of heated discussion in the debate that followed the Asian crisis in 1997. Most economists and financial operators, in fact, concentrated their analyses of the causes of the crisis on debtor countries, that is, on the conditions of credit demand. After years of talk about the "Asian miracle," immediately following the explosion of the crisis the Asian economies were accused of everything (lack of transparency, clientelism, poor knowledge of financial mechanisms, etc.). On the contrary, it is fundamental that we search for the first cause of the crisis, of the Asian crisis just like the Mexican crisis of 1994–1995 and the EMS crisis of 1993, *in the center countries* because they are the ones that determine the dynamics of global financial markets.

For neoliberal economists the reasons for the crisis were to be found essentially in faulty information and in the absence of restrictions on countries that make use of international capital. For this reason, in December 1998 organizations such as the OECD and the World Trade Organization (WTO) tried, without success thanks to a vast opposition movement, to effect a total liberalization of direct foreign investment, under the aegis of a *multilateral agreement on investment*, a stranglehold agreement which would have left emerging countries on the receiving end of international capital investments without any autonomy whatsoever.

Every monetary and financial crisis has its specific characteristics, but all of them fall within this interpretive scheme of the dynamics of the new financial imperialism. In the case of the Asian crisis, what contributed to the collapse of a whole group of economies already experiencing a decline in productivity gains and internal political consensus, was the system of fixed parity between Asian currencies and the dollar, a system which caused an increase in the trade deficit when the dollar appreciated and world trade stalled. The stubborn defense of parity with the dollar rapidly emptied the cash drawers of the Asian central banks until there was nothing to do but devalue.

Every crisis is characterized by the reflux of capital toward Western countries. The role of movements of *short-term capital* in destabilizing the global financial system was to be much debated over the next couple of years, and gave birth to an international political movement (ATTAC, Association for the Taxation of Financial Transactions to Aid Citizens), with the objective of introducing a tax (the Tobin tax) on profits realized on speculative movements—in the short term—of capital, thus providing governments of developed countries with substantial tax revenues with which to combat global poverty.

It is nevertheless essential to understand that these short-term shifts of capital are the product of the "price revolution," of disinflation as effected by post-Fordist modes of production, and by the financialization of savings. These two phenomena were what gave rise to *pension fund capitalism*, in which institutional investors are forced to adopt an increasingly aggressive approach to asset management in the search for higher returns with which to satisfy both the demands of ongoing operations and the payout of pension benefits. In pension fund capitalism the aging of the population and the reduction in the number of salaried employees are important contributing factors in explaining the gradual shift of the pension system from the principle of distribution (the 1st pillar of social security) to the principle of capitalization (the 2nd and 3rd pillars). The effect of disinflation on the value of pension benefits, however, is equally important. For pension funds, paying out benefits after a long period of deflation means paying benefits with *revalued* money. For retired people, it means being paid benefits which, although sheltered from inflation, must still make their way through the inferno of the financial markets. A compromise, a "post-Fordist social contract," between the representatives of labor and the managers of pension funds should be reachable somewhere around the halfway point between short-term returns, more remunerative but also more destabilizing, and long-term returns, less remunerative but less destructive of the social conditions of economic growth. "This could be," Michael Aglietta writes, "a future prospect for western European unions. They are destined by their history to overcome the corporative interests of single categories of workers in order to represent the needs of the wage-earners as a whole. Wage-earner funds could provide them with the means for influencing profitability norms. Instead of a maximum short-term return, they could demand a guaranteed long term rate of profitability, in exchange for stability of control over the company" (Aglietta, 2001).

The role of pension funds in the workings of global finance is one of those internal contradictions of developed countries which radiate outward to peripheral countries, destructuring local economies and preventing them from restructuring in accordance with the principle of self-determination. Furthermore, it is a contradiction which has become more explosive as disinflation has dragged interest rates down in countries such as Japan which, in the face of the revaluation of the yen in 1999 and the resulting risk of a decline in exports, couldn't very well make further reductions in interest rates already very close to zero.

Another of these contradictions can be seen in the policy of the IMF, a policy which aims to apply the same cure to the crises of countries which are very different from one another. In the case of the Asian crisis, however, the IMF's response turned out to be not only late but ineffective and, in fact, the Asian economies managed to recover on their own between 1998 and 2000 by following local policies contrary to those proposed by the Fund: by lowering interest rates, that is, through (Keynesian) expansive deficit spending, Asian countries stimulated the recovery on their own and made themselves attractive once again to foreign investment.

The IMF pursues macroeconomic strategies that are supposed to be valid for all kinds of local economies, without taking account of their specific characteristics. Peripheral countries, on the other hand, if they want to ensure themselves a margin of self-determination, have to find a way to exploit their specific differences. And they can do this, at least partially, only by slowing down the process of liberalization promoted by western countries. This has been done, for example, by Malaysia, which since 1998 has placed strict controls on the movement of foreign capital out of the country, controls which are necessary to prevent capital flight, but certainly not sufficient to bring about real democratic reform on the national level.

The analysis of the global effects of the current crisis of the New Economy makes it possible to update the center-periphery model. First, with regard to the model and to the entire tradition of studies of 20th century imperialism, it must be noted that, in the course of the expansive phase and the crisis of the New Economy, the driving force behind the movements of capital into and out of peripheral countries was not interest rates but the performance of financial markets. This is a very important difference which signals a change in the underlying logic of the hierarchy of global markets. The leading role in today's global economy is played not by nation-states but by their financial markets, which in turn are driven by mechanisms, such as the operation of a *public convention*, which can easily funtion outside the boundaries of nation-states.

Second, and again with regard to the center-periphery model, it should be noted how the New Economy functioned to generate an enormous deficit in the current account of the United States, counterbalanced in turn by the influx of capital and savings from the rest of the world, especially from Europe, to American financial markets. The US current account deficit allowed Asian and Latin American countries to maintain high export levels, but the elevated value of the dollar caused by the influx of foreign capital, particularly European capital, signaled Europe's *dependence* on the New Economy model. Moreover, this came about in a period in which Europe had finally provided itself with a European currency, the Euro, whose primary historical objective had always been to protect Europe from the influence of the dollar and American monetary policy in order to ensure itself an economic and social development which respects its specific continental and regional characteristics.

Add to all this the price of oil which, between the end of 1999 and the end of 2001, varied wildly from 20 to over 30 dollars a barrel. It has been said that the crisis of 2000 was the first oil crisis without a name. According to Leonardo Maugeri (a high-ranking manager at ENI, the Italian oil and natural gas company, and the author of *Petrolio. Storie di falsi miti*, 2001), the real cause of crude oil price volatility is not to be found in OPEC's pricing policy but in the kind of crude oil required by the United States (light sweet crude, whose supply is limited compared to other grades of crude). "It makes less and less sense, therefore, to speak in general terms about the balance of oil supply and demand, whereas it is very important to understand whether, in any given period, the crude available on the international markets corresponds to the quality of crude required by those who will have to consume it. What happened in 2000, for example, was a short circuit in the nominally abundant supply of crude [the consequence of an error in judgment by OPEC, which had decided in the fall of 1997 to increase production just as the crisis was exploding in Southeast Asia, the region that in recent years had recorded the strongest increases in the rate of oil consumption] and a very high demand for some special grades of crude whose supply, on the contrary, was quite scarce." Keeping in mind that the United States consumes 20 million barrels a day while it produces only 8 million, it is highly probable that the United States will continue to be a factor in oil price instability. And this regardless of the choices of George W. Bush who has been intent on exploiting the energy emergency to restore power to producers (by allowing drilling in regions such as Alaska and authorizing the construction of nuclear power plants), thus undermining any possible alternative energy policy.

The deregulation of the energy sector has brought back the "old dangers" of the 1970s in an economy that over the last twenty years has nevertheless steadily reduced energy consumption (relative to economic growth rates) by expanding the service sector and investing in energy conservation. Naturally, the price for all this has been paid by consumers in western countries but also in emerging countries where industrialization has increased dependence on imported raw materials. In the United States, according to a Harris poll of car owners, 46% had to cut down on their consumption of goods and services in order to pay higher prices for gasoline; of these 46%, 72% had cut down on weekend trips, 53% had reduced vacation spending, and 31% had put off buying a new car (half of whom said they wanted to buy an energy-saving car).

The decline in the price of crude in the second half of 2001 is not to be attributed to the declining demand from American drivers but rather to the increased supply coming from Russian production under the direction of the American multinationals. For the first time in its history the OPEC cartel runs the risk of losing its power over the world supply of crude (and this is one of the fundamental aspects of Putin's change in strategy).

Six months into 2001 the dollar, as a consequence of the prolonged crisis in the United States, showed signs of weakening to the advantage of the Euro, which was able to ease up on its hitherto absurdly anti-inflationary monetary policy, but to the disadvantage of the yen, which in exactly this same period saw the Japanese Central Bank engaged yet again in an attempt to stimulate internal demand by reducing interest rates. To be sure, the countries of Southeast Asia and Latin America suffered heavy consequences from this new (compared to the years of the Clinton administration) weak dollar policy, an autarchic policy whose objective was to reinforce the financial markets by favoring American exports in order to offset the decline in internal demand for capital goods.

Since the Federal Reserve's repeated reductions in interest rates starting in 2001 failed to achieve a lasting recovery of the financial markets, an easy credit policy on the part of the American monetary authorities risked sending the dollar into a downward spiral that could have compromised any hope of putting an end to the crisis. In order to avoid a devaluation of the dollar while financing the current account deficit, which since 1999 had been growing at the rate of $30 billion a month, the American markets had to attract $1 billion *a day* from around the world. But if global investors started selling the American securities in which they had invested, the devaluation of the currency risked giving rise to a vicious circle of weakening financial markets accompanied by a free fall in the value of the dollar.

The threat of a capital exodus from American markets was seen as particularly dangerous for *bonds* issued by big corporations such as GM and Ford. In just the first five months of 2001, the big corporations (together with public agencies) attracted something like

$190 billion, an amount greater than the current account deficit accumulated in the same period.

To better understand what was at stake here, it is worth recalling that at the beginning of February 2000 Bill Clinton decided to complete paying off the entire national debt two years in advance (by the end of 2013) by using the budget surpluses generated from tax revenues, revenues which by the beginning of 1998 were greater than expenditures thanks, in addition to increasing profits and growing upper income brackets, to income taxes generated by the stock market boom (in the Unites States taxes on *capital gains* were then 17% on the average). Retiring the national debt in just a few years would mean reducing the volume of government bonds offered on the market (there would be a scarcity of debt obligations issued by the Treasury to finance long-term investments). Since pension funds and insurance companies invest part of their portfolios in long-term bonds to cover their long-term commitments, there was a race to purchase bonds which were on their way to being drastically reduced. This explains the increase in bond prices and, conversely, the decline in their yields (in long-term interest rates).

The technical aspects of what happened shouldn't distract our attention from the political substance of the operation. Essentially, what we're dealing with is a continuation of the neoliberal policy of the "empty coffers," or the "poor State"; the use of surplus revenues not to consolidate the welfare state but to reduce taxes on income and capital or, as in this case, to payoff the public debt accumulated over several decades. The State's empty coffers, that is, serve as a disciplinary device: as long as there are debts, as long as the coffers are empty, no new spending, only cuts in social programs. In its comment on Clinton's decision, even the "Economist," a steadfast supporter of antidebt extremism, wondered what sense it made for a business not to have debts if it then fails due to the breakdown of its assembly line. What is the point of retiring public debt if in order to do it you have to eliminate spending for education, public transportation, and research: investments without which economic growth itself is compromised?

We can begin to answer this question by recalling that 50 years ago American railroad bonds functioned as a *benchmark*, the indicator of reference for investors, exactly as, since the Keynesian revolution of the welfare state long-term government bonds (30 year notes) had functioned as indicators of the trend in interest rates.

Underlying the decision to shorten the period for the retirement of its public debt was the desire of the United States to replace government bonds with *private* bonds in the strategic role of market indicators. Already in 1999, while the volume of treasury notes was decreasing by $87 billion, the volume of long-term debt securities of the big corporations was increasing by $461 billion. But by reducing public debt even more rapidly than planned, the government of the Unites States revealed its intention, at the beginning of 2000, to undermine the benchmark role of public debt, imposing on the rest of the world the long-term debt of the most powerful American corporations.

An uncontrolled devaluation of the dollar, both cause and effect of the exodus of capital from American government bonds, therefore, threatened to undermine the strategy of privatizing the benchmark indicators of the global markets. With the crisis of the New Economy the future of neoliberal global policies was really up for grabs.

Even with a stronger Euro, Europe was not capable of replacing the United States in its role as the engine of economic recovery, or as the importer of the recession of the countries of Southeast Asia. The crisis of the American New Economy, in fact, strongly deflated the new European financial markets (the markets for high-tech securities), especially in Germany, thus making it impossible to *replicate* in Europe the American model of the New Economy and the global conditions which brought it into being in the 1990s.

It is no coincidence that Germany, which in 1993 had designed the Maastrict Stability Pact and imposed it on the member-states of the European Union (as the condition for its consent to replace the mark with the Euro by 1999), now felt the need to ease up on the restrictive and compulsory conditions of the agreement. In a crisis that appeared as though it might go on for quite some time, Germany's objective (as the country that produced 30% of the EU's GDP and thus had been hit hardest by the crisis of the New Economy), was to establish public spending caps and to act to stimulate the economy *only* on the fiscal front (fewer tax cuts in recessive periods and, vice-versa, larger tax cuts in periods of income growth), thus avoiding reductions in public spending in periods of greater social need (unemployment, poverty, etc.). An idea which certainly responded to the needs, not only of Germany but also of countries like France, Italy, Austria and Portugal (all countries which already in 2001 were no longer in a position to respect the conditions of the Maastricht Pact), but which, by leaving member states total discretion on fiscal policy, ended up defeating the very purposes of the pact. In other words, the crisis of the New Economy was *also* the crisis of European unification as it had been pursued over the course of the 1990s through restrictive social policies and restrictive monetary policies on the part of the European Central Bank.

What is striking about this phase of the New Economy's cycle is that it was the first international crisis to be completely *synchronized* (along with the United States, economic indicators in all countries, European, Latin American, Asian, were negative). But what is even more worrisome is the *speed* and *breadth* of the crisis and this derived from a series of structural factors.

First, world trade had come to represent 25% of world economic output, twice as much as in 1970. A large part of this trade involved the United States: in 2000 exports to the United States accounted for 25% of the Mexican economy, 32% of Canada's, and 40% of Asian output excluding Japan. The combination of a strong dollar and economic weakness in the rest of the world could have brought about a 5 to 10% drop in American exports of goods and services, thus dashing all hopes of achieving the 3% growth thought to be necessary for America to overcome the current crisis.

Second, the globalization of finance and investments, which is to say the fact that the same investors and the same global banks operate indifferently on all the world's financial markets, means that what happens in one corner of the globe has immediate consequences elsewhere. Already in 1980, for example, the speculative bubble of the Japanese real estate and stock markets had an immediate impact on the United States. Throughout the 1990s, the volatility of the Nasdaq generated symmetrical waves of volatility in Europe and Asia. In 2001, the Argentine recession was pushing up interest rates in Brazil, Mexico, and South Africa, nullifying the hope of growth in those countries.

Finally, the growth of multinational companies in recent years had intensified the *connectivity* of the global economy. When a multinational enterprise achieves good results, it tends to increase investments and employment *everywhere*—even in underperforming regions and product lines. And the same is true in the opposite case: when a multinational starts to feel under siege by bad performance in several of its divisions, the tendency is to withdraw on all fronts at the same time.

On the basis of these "updates" of the center-periphery model we can propose an initial, partial, conclusion. The New Economy, both in terms of financialization and the explosion of the high-tech sector, has modified the world's financial-monetary circuit so that the center countries, especially the United States, have lost their relative decisional autonomy (in monetary policy and in the determination of the flow of goods) which, in the past, in the imperialistic model, allowed them to regulate the domestic business cycle by exporting their internal contradictions to peripheral countries.

The New Economy, to recall the thesis of Toni Negri and Michael Hardt (2000), marks in all probability the crisis of 20th century imperialism and the advent of the *empire*, the world system of the nonsubject, the non-State, the nonplace, a headless system which has absorbed all residual external spaces (external to the global circuit of capital), thus depriving itself of the very possibility of exporting its internal contradictions outside of the economic circuit.

Indeed, globalization has inscribed itself in the constitution of the world market, defined by Marx as capital's greatest historical task. This is the element of *continuity* of globalization within the historical development of the world market, the generation of the exploitation of the work-force on a planetary scale as the "precondition and result of capitalistic production." In this historical trajectory, the growth of foreign trade and global money contribute to the globalization of capital as *social relationship*, a relationship articulated in the international division of labor and in the hierarchical relationships among nation-States.

The current phase of globalization is marked by a world market undergoing a total recomposition based on a number of factors: the intensification of information flows; industrial dislocation and concentration; the internationalization of the goods and services markets ("global village"); the financialization of processes of accumulation (the multiplication of securities markets); the dismantling of the welfare state, and the redefinition of the specific weights of the various economic powers. In the process of this globalization of the capitalistic relations of production, the technical division of labor converges in space more rapidly than the cost of reproduction of the work force, so that salary differentials are used for the reticular construction of enterprises on a transnational scale in the name of "concentration without centralization," of flexible decentralization controlled and coordinated by the enterprises of center countries (Harrison, 1999).

The world economy has never been only an inter-national economy, which is to say, an economy strongly oriented toward the outside but whose main entities are national economies. The determination of *asymmetrical relationships*, directed by the international monetary and financial system, has always represented, even in the times of the *gold standard*, the *global* element of international economic growth (De Cecco, 1998; Strange, 1999; Krugman, 2001). Nor is it unimaginable, contrary to the model of the purely international economy, that there could develop a totally globalized economy, a world-system in which the single national economies would be subsumed and rearticulated within the system by processes and transactions completely autonomous with respect to the social roots of local economies. In globalization the *local* (metropolitan) *and regional determination* of the production and distribution of wealth maintains and even conflictually reinforces the inter-national dimension within the global economy (Sassen, 1998).

The hybridization between the inter-national dimension and the global vocation of world economic development explains the paradoxical results of the evolutionist analyses of scholars such as Hirst and Thompson (1997), according to whom, the world economy was comparatively more "global" in the period 1870– 1914 (greater intensity of movements of capital for direct foreign investment and greater migrational flows), and more "inter-national" in the period between 1980 and the 1990s (greater concentration of production and logistics in the countries of origin of multinational corporations).

The merit of such "continuist" interpretations of globalization consists, rather than in their proposals to reinforce the institutional management and the inter-national regulation of the world economy, in their demonstration that analyses of globalization which do not focus on changes in *modes of production* and transformations of the nature of work are bound to arrive at an impasse. The consequences of globalization on the lives of people *in developed countries*, in addition to those in poor countries and developing countries (Sennett, 1999; Bauman, 1999), the specification of movements of capital and of the new financial capital from the point of view of workers' savings (pension benefits) and of the *financialization of household economies* (Aglietta, 1995), and analyses of new forms of organized violence in the global age (Kaldor, 1999), are interpretations of globalization which aim to identify the elements of *discontinuity* in the historical process of the creation of the world market. In the post-Fordist growth model the sphere of the circulation of goods is directly subsumed by the production and enhancement of capital, which in turn defines in *bio-political terms* the modalities of control, regulation, and reproduction of the work force on a planetary scale (see Hardt and Negri, 2000).

The withering of the relatively autonomous monetary regulation of the business cycle, the subordination of the polices of the central banks, and in the first place of the Federal Reserve, to the dynamics of the securities markets and the revaluation of pension benefits, are the other facet of the direct subsumption of circulation to the production of social wealth. The diversion of pension funds and collective savings from the debt securities of the welfare state to the stocks and bonds of the securities markets embodies the omnivorous nature of the post-Fordist production of wealth, the "putting to work" of aging itself through the cancellation of the Keynesian separation between savings and investment (Marazzi, 1998).

The *linguistic nature* of post-Fordist labor and the *virtualization* of technico-productive processes (digitalization of production, acceleration of information flows and the superimposition of the product and service dimensions of goods) comport a radical change in the framework of the production of wealth on a world scale. From this perspective, globalization can be defined as the passage from the classical dynamics of imperialism to the logic of *Empire*. Globalization as empire is the worldwide organization of the subsumption of circulation into production, the "putting to work" of the *life* of the work force in the global factory. The monetary twist to this real subsumption is *disinflation*, noninflationary growth, the production of a structural excess of social wealth, which the traditional maneuvering of interest rates in an effort to regulate the business cycle is no longer able to manage without aggravating the instability of the global financial system. In the globalization of the empire, financial crises are *circumscribed*, but this takes nothing away from the gravity of their effects on local populations. To the exportation of goods and capital characteristic of historical imperialism, globalization has added the exportation of collective savings in the search for returns high enough to offset the monetary effects of noninflationary growth (banking disintermediation as the result of the progressive reduction of interest rates). In this process, global financial and monetary instability is determined by short-term movements of capital, movements increasingly less instrumental to speculation *in itself*, but increasingly determined by the aging rates and life cycles of center-country populations. The demographic pressure of countries on the periphery of the empire increases with the increase in subsumption of the real economy.

The passage from imperialism to empire threatens the stability of the international division of labor and the asymmetries between center and periphery as worldwide flows of capital and the unequal redistribution of wealth meet resistance from the *body* of the global work force, from its *multiplicity*. In order to function, the empire must exercise control over the reproduction of the work force in such a way as to erase diversity (ethnic, religious, cultural) generating *blur communities, communities of the indistinct*. The financial logic typical of imperial globalization *balkanizes* the body of the global work force at the same time that it dictates the economic policies of nation-States.

The exemplarity of the "humanitarian war" in the Balkans consists in its having highlighted the contradiction between global financial policies—the measures taken by the IMF and the international financial community which, starting in the early 1980s, had led to the progressive dissolution of the institutional framework of the former Yugoslavia, by generating high rates of unemployment and poverty—and the explosion of the multiplicity of the body of the Balkan work force in the form of ethnic warfare. The *humanitarian* nature of the NATO intervention revealed the centrality of the body of the work force, the centrality of *taking care of one's body* in all of its dimensions in the imperial age of globalization, the unresolved conflict between the supranational determination of processes of accumulation and the ontology of the collective body, its irreducible multiplicity (Habermas, 1999). In the empire of globalization, human rights are akin to one of its immaterial elements, the *service* component of products, with the difference that for products the immaterial element defines relationships of reciprocity, whereas in the case of human rights the immaterial element defines them as *concepts without bodies, linguistic acts* which are realized by *dissolving* bonds of reciprocity, by balkanizing the collective nature of the human body.

The Cycle According to Mandel

The risk of moving from the virtuous circle of the American economy of the 1990s to an *internet depression*, with devastating consequences for the entire world economy, depended in large part on the *political* management of the business cycle. This was the thesis of Michael Mandel, one of the most convinced theorists of the New Economy. In his *The Coming Internet Depression* (2000), Mandel argued that the New Economy was about to go through a palindromic movement of expansion and contraction. "Unfortunately, the odds of a bad policy mistake are too high for comfort. There is still widespread disagreement about the nature of the New Economy, making [cycle management] errors [by the monetary authorities] more likely." The turning point of the cycle, according to Mandel, depends on the Federal Reserve's reaction to the return of inflation induced by the reduction in productivity caused by a decline in investments in *high tech*. This thesis is debatable, as we have just seen, but it deserves our attention because it contains some new elements with respect to the dynamics of the cycle and the crisis.

In Mandel's view, an inversion of the curve of expansion into an economic recession is possible because the New Economy cannot be ascribed only to the information revolution and its destabilizing effects on the cycle. The computerization of the chain of production and distribution of goods and services has certainly contributed to improving inventory monitoring, and thus to avoiding an excess of production with respect to effective demand. The combination of growing productivity and intense competition, on the other hand, has helped to keep inflation under control, allowing the Federal Reserve to ensure continuing growth without having to increase interest rates excessively.

The problem is that the New Economy is more than a technological revolution; it is also a financial revolution, and this is what radically changes the logic of the cycle compared to the cycle of the Keynesian-Fordist economy. To be sure, even in the Old Economy the end of the expansion phase was marked by the turning off of the credit faucet to businesses, which happened gradually as the cycle moved toward full employment. When consumer spending slowed, accompanied by a corresponding slowdown in companies' repayment of debts to the banking system, investors could sense the danger of a crisis of overproduction.

But in the New Economy the *risk reassessment* that leads to the recessive phase as creditors withdraw from the real economy has changed, thanks to the increasingly central role played by *venture capital*. In the 1990s venture capitalists provided the financial leverage for the innovation that gave birth to the internet *Dot Com* companies and to the processes of business restructuring that then radiated throughout the entire economy. If technology is the engine of the new economy, finance is the gasoline. It is a finance very sensitive to swings in stock prices, which raises the risk of its withdrawal from the markets, especially from the tech markets, with depressive consequences for the sector that has driven overall growth thanks to increases in productivity generated by investments in technology. This is exactly what happened in the course of 2000–2001.

The mechanisms for financing technological innovation that allowed venture capital to grow immeasurably (in 1988 the overall amount of U.S. venture capital was $5 billion, in 2000 it had risen to $100 billion, or some 40% of total capital invested in research and development) can be explained by the Marxian concept of *general intellect*, with the added specification that we mentioned at the beginning of our discussion. The term applies to widespread knowledge historically determined by the development of the productive force of scientific knowledge, but with a difference with respect to what Marx wrote in the *Grundrisse*, which is that this knowledge is no longer crystallized in fixed capital, in machines, but is nurtured only by living labor.

The entrepreneurial conjugation of the *general intellect* consists in transforming communication into an assembly line, turning speed and productive and distributive interconnection into commodities. Having assumed the form of living scientific knowledge, the *general intellect*, in order to become entrepreneurial, has to be financed from *outside* the classic channels of basic research, outside, that is, of the R&D programs of big corporations, government agencies, and universities. Today a dollar of venture capital stimulates from three to five more patents and licenses than a dollar spent on R&D.

The capacity of living labor, which generates innovation without fixing itself in machines and special infrastructures, to gain access to financing, allows us to understand both the impressive increase in capital in search of ideas to invest in (increasingly less capital is absorbed in costly investments in infrastructure; excluding transportation, investments in cost-reducing technologies represent 63% of total spending on equipment), as well as the destabilizing nature of this particular way of financing the *general intellect*.

The dispersion and the speed of distribution of the innovation specific to the *general intellect* correspond to the search for short-term profits that characterizes the category of *venture capitalists*. The combination of new innovative enterprises and their financing with venture capital accelerates the diffusion of restructuring innovation throughout all sectors of the economy, from the automobile industry to telecommunications and health care, from real estate to public services, from the distribution chain to the single retail outlet. It is a mistake to think of the explosion of tech stocks as a simple speculative bubble, even though the speculative component certainly contributed to the massive diversion of worldwide savings to these stocks, upsetting the normal application of innovations to production and distribution systems.

Their lack of tangible physical capital and their dependence on future sales makes it especially difficult to evaluate virtual *Dot Com* enterprises on the basis of such Fordist indicators as the *price/ earnings ratio*, constructed experientially on the basis of historical regularities of accumulation.

Once they have been launched on the market, information products are reproduced at no cost precisely because they are intangible. The rate of piracy and cloning ensures, despite copyright protections, the rapid diffusion of ever new products. Their real economic interest lies in achieving mass use of their products, which requires a certain level of initiation on the part of potential consumers. The example of the first public libraries at the end of the 18th century can help us to understand this apparently paradoxical phenomenon. At first, the opening of the first public libraries was seen by book publishers as a serious threat to their profits. But afterwards, free access to reading led to the massification of the publishing market well beyond the initial portion of readers/consumers to whom publishers sold their books, as they exercised a monopoly based on the cost of production. We now know that the monopolistic control of book readers is no longer exercised on the basis of the costs of production and sales but on control over distribution, of the organization of access to knowledge in general.

The tension between the criteria for evaluating the efficiency of old and new enterprises, between enterprises that have tangible capital and enterprises that don't, creating their profits by virtue of owning intellectual property, has to do with the *time* difference in the creation of markets, the time necessary for the diffusion of products which, *in order to become commodities*, must produce their own consumers. It is precisely this time difference that literally explodes evaluation models for new enterprises, forcing the market to devalue *Dot Com* companies after just a few years unless they demonstrate that they know how to make tangible profits.

Even today, despite the decline in share prices of stocks listed on the Nasdaq, the most important *Dot Com* companies would have to realize extraordinarily high average profits over many years in order to justify the current price of their shares. The incommensurability of the New Economy with respect to the Old Economy makes the financial markets even more self-referential than they were in the Keynesian era. As we have already seen, the markets are spheres of subjective behavior where what counts is not what the individual investor believes but what he believes the others believe; markets are places in which economic rationality is manifested in the work of rumors, chit-chat, public opinion. In the financial universe "cognitive activity is directed toward generality and toward common reference points," which is to say, toward the Keynesian conventions of old" (Orléan, 1999, p.79).

The financialization of society is now such that someone has coined the phrase "ownership individualism" to indicate our all being "minority shareholders." This is one of those *socially necessary appearances* alluded to by Marx to account for our being there even when we are not (for his time Marx indicated the *salary* as one of these socially necessary appearances). It can legitimately be asserted that in the latter half of the 1990s the idea of a digitalized society, with liberating effects on ways of living and working, became a socially shared convention. True or false as it may be, there is no doubt that this convention has been the driving force for real processes of transformation.

In these conditions, the crisis is the only realistic way of assessing the *market's regulatory power* over New Economy enterprises. The crisis forces investors to redirect capital on the basis of the Schumpeterian distinction between technological innovation and market innovation. The crisis reveals the existence of a *digital overproduction*, an excess of innovations with respect to the market's capacity to absorb them; with respect to its effective demand. A "digital cornucopia," an excessive supply of digital goods, already latent in the expansion phase, but which the recession has taken charge of marketizing by devaluing all innovative capital which is not transformed immediately into profit (see, Schrage, 2000).

In his theory of the cycle of the New Economy, Mandel posits inflation as the starting point of the crisis: prices rise when investments in high tech decline, venture capital financing dries up, and the economy slows down. This is the weakest part of Mandel's theory of the cycle.

"On the downward swing of the tech cycle, the economy will paradoxically become much more inflation-prone. When productivity growth slows and investment falls off, it will become harder for companies to absorb wage increases without raising prices. And large companies will have less reason to restrain themselves because they will have less fear of competition from startups. That suggests the downturn is likely to see an increase in the pricing power of large firms, especially in the early years of the decline" (Mandel, p. 58).

Apart from the decline in competition, according to Mandel, the return of inflation will probably be caused by a slowdown in innovation. "In the second half of the 1990s, rapidly falling prices for software and information technology equipment sliced about a half percentage point off the inflation rate (as measure by the GD deflator). As the rate of innovation slows, it's likely that tech prices will fall at a slower rate. That could add significantly to inflation all by itself" (*ibid*, p. 59).

Together, the decline in competition from rival companies and the slowdown in the rate of innovation allow large companies to raise prices in order to combat the shrinkage of profits caused by decreases in productivity. The Fed, fearing inflation, raises interest rates, thus aggravating the recessive phase with further disinvestment in high tech.

Apart from the fact that a decrease in demand for capital goods tends to *reduce* the threat of inflation, Mandel's theory is debatable because it considers variations (positive or negative) in productivity essentially from the point of view of the application of new technologies. It lacks, that is, an analysis of productivity from the point of view of *living labor*, taking into account the change in working conditions resulting from the reorganization of the cycle of production and distribution (*just in time*, inventory monitoring now twice as high as sales compared to three times ten years ago), the fact that in the New Economy labor productivity is, like salaries, a dramatically flexible *adjustment variable* that can increase even without the continuous application of new technologies.

A fine example in this regard is the book by Bill Lessard and Steve Baldwin, *Net Slaves: True Tales of Working the Web* (2000), which for the first time attempts a class analysis or better, a caste analysis of the working universe of the web: the *New Media Caste System*. The authors identify eleven categories of workers in the social order of the web, each with its own detailed description of personal-socio-anthropological and income characteristics: from the lowest category of the web *garbagemen* who work endless hours cleaning and compiling programs, responding to customer complaints, inserting and extracting components from the hardware, to the cops or *streetwalkers*, whose work consists in repressing the reticular manifestations of sexual stimuli, to the social workers who spend their time managing all kinds of online conversations, to the *fry cooks* who fry the lives of programmers to keep them on schedule, up to the new, and few, *robber barons*, not to forget the *moles* or microentrepreneurs.

In the factory of the web, employment is highly unstable; people change jobs 3 or 4 times a year. There are no fixed working hours, and no social services. Social relationships are, as the hierarchy implies, conducted along caste lines, with the difference that here the rate of upward and downward mobility is extremely high. Productivity increases without any consideration for the effects on the private lives of workers: "a complete absence of social life, terrible eating habits, no physical exercise, cigarettes by the thousands, recurring nervous breakdowns and, not least, hemorrhoids" (Lessard and Baldwin, 2000, p. 246).

There is no reason to suppose that the disinflationary forces at work in the expansion phase of the cycle cease to operate in the contraction phases of production and application of new web technologies. And the proof lies in the devaluation of the lives of the 9-10% of working Americans who, directly or indirectly, make up the wage-earning *general intellect.*

Assuming it doesn't set off the process of internal inflation which according to Mandel would lead directly to a depression, the increase in risk aversion typical of the downturn phase of the New Economy business cycle has nevertheless had deleterious effects on those emerging countries which have recently had recourse to foreign capital and which, like Argentina, have completely abandoned the public pension system in favor of a system based on capitalization. In this case the increase in the *spread* (the difference between yields on comparable risk debt securities) has been very high, to the point that the cost of the slowdown amounts to 1.5–2% of the GDP of emerging countries.

From the point of view of the *political* analysis of the cycle, which is really the dimension that interests Mandel, the convergence between the devaluation of life in the Center and in the Periphery counts for more than an unproven universal existential condition of the *general intellect.* A study by the Employment Policy

Institute, *The State of Working America* (2000–1, Washington, D.C., see www.epinet.org) demonstrates, contrary to a lot of claims in recent years, that from 1995 to 2001 no more than 25% of the active American population works in conditions similar to those of the *netslaves* of the New Economy. The trend would seem instead to be toward an *expansion* of *dependent employment*, although in forms totally different from Fordist dependent employment. This doesn't change the fact that the polarization of incomes has intensified ("In 1999, an American manager worked half a week to earn what an average wage-earner earned in 52 weeks," compared to the two and a half weeks of 1965), as has the number of annual work hours.

Finally, from the point of view of job creation, development of the technology sector, productivity rates, and the resistance of the welfare state, the superiority of the American New Economy with respect to the countries of Northern Europe remains to be demonstrated, as shown by a study of the National Bureau of Economic Research (*The US Economic Model at Y2K: Lodestar for Advanced Capitalism?*, edited by R. Freeman of Harvard University and the London School of Economics, www.nber.org).

3

The Return of Surplus Value

The Economic Circuit and the Monetization of Surplus Value

The striking thing about the dynamics of the New Economy business cycle is how fast it builds up excess inventories of unsold goods as soon as demand starts to decline, particularly the demand for *high tech* capital goods. Furthermore, this comes on the heels of years of organizational restructuring inspired by the Japanese *just in time* and *zero stock* techniques which, according to the post-Fordist manuals, should, if not totally eliminate, at least greatly reduce the risks of overproduction.

The question of excess inventories has been associated by many observers with the perverse effects of *overtrading*: the more fever-pitched the rising phase of the cycle as an effect of increased consumption fueled by debt, the more violent the recessive demand phase and, therefore, the higher the volumes of unsold stock. This is an old story that has to do with the difficult transition from *extensive* to *intensive* enlarged reproduction, the transition, that is, from enlarged reproduction in which the two sectors (consumer goods and investment goods) grow in parallel and mostly at the same rate, to enlarged reproduction in which growth is limited only to the investment goods (means of production) sector, whereas demand for consumer goods is constant or, as when the economy approaches full employment, gradually declining (to the extent that the marginal increments of consumption induced by new hiring are smaller).

From the point of view of Marxian critical analysis, the role of overtrading in the expansive phase of the cycle, the creation, that is, of *additional demand* with respect to demand created by the payment of wages and salaries in both sectors—consumer goods and investment goods—demonstrates that the creation of surplus value does not lead in itself to the creation of demand sufficient for its realization. The capital cycle, in other words, is structurally unbalanced *ex ante*, so that only exportation or public deficit spending or, as in the New Economy, liquidity created by the workings of the financial markets, is able to ensure the continuity of the business cycle. If this were not the case, declining demand should bring supply and demand back into equilibrium. But, on the contrary, *as soon as* demand begins to decline, unsold stocks start to show up, which means there is some amount of unrealizable value (surplus value)! It appears, therefore, that it may be useful to take another look at the Marxian analysis of the cycle and the crisis.

It must be recalled that in classical economics, as opposed to the neoclassical school, the functioning of the economy is represented by something called the *economic circuit*, a circuit which links production and consumption in their various phases. Volume II of *Capital* contains Marx's best description of the economic circuit, a concept first developed by the Physiocrats in the middle of the 18th century. The economic circuit is important as a representation of the capitalist economy because it provides a description of the temporal sequentiality of production and reproduction, as well as the circularity that links the payment and spending of wages (Fig. 1).

Figure 1: The Economic Circuit

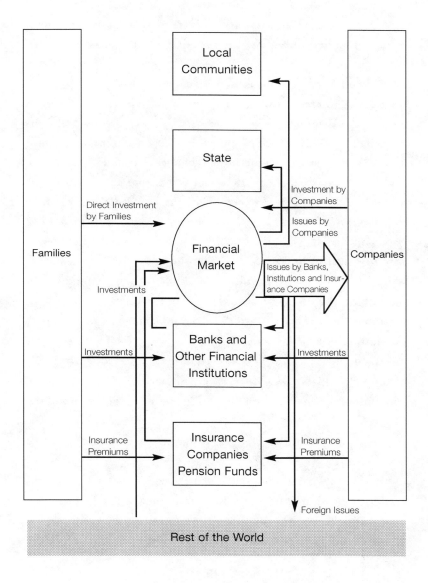

As is well known, in volume II of *Capital* Marx first analyzes simple reproduction, in which all surplus value is (unproductively) consumed by the capitalist. Subsequently, Marx analyzes enlarged reproduction, in which part of the *realized*, that is to say *sold*, surplus value is invested to enlarge the productive process itself and the volume of employment.

One important feature of the analysis, which is responsible for a series of errors and ambiguities in the Marxist tradition, is that in the diagrams used as the basis for Marx's argument the exchanges between goods produced in the consumer goods sector and the investment sector are exchanges effected in terms of *exchange value* (that is, of the social work time contained in the goods), and—an aspect which confirms the centrality of these exchanges in Marx's analysis, in terms of *use value* (of subsistence goods and capital goods), but *not* in terms of the money necessary to execute the exchange. "The money on one side," Marx writes in chapter XXI of volume II, "calls forth expanded reproduction on the other, because the possibility for it exists without the money. For money in itself is not an element of actual reproduction" (Marx, 1907, p. 572).

In the diagrams, in fact, the argument is developed in terms of simple circulation, C-M-C', where money (M) performs, if you will, an evanescent function as a bridge between the commodities C, C', C", ... What counts here is the commensurability of the commodities, the mere reference to money as a measure of value is sufficient.

In one passage of volume II Marx is concerned with the conversion/realization of surplus value into money, where he posits the hypothesis that the money lacking for overall actual production is supplied annually by the gold producer. But the solution of the gold producer, although valid with regard to simple circulation (C-M-C'), *does not* respond in any way to the central problem of capital circulation M-C-M'. Here the conversion of surplus value into money is fundamental for the continuity of circulation. In capital circulation the problem is no longer the quantity of money but the quantity of monetary incomes.

On the other hand, when in discussing his diagrams of reproduction Marx interrogates himself on the "reproduction of monetary material," he demonstrates a clear understanding of the difference between simple circulation and capital circulation: "Take it that the entire production belonged to the laborers, so that their surplus-labor were done for themselves, not for the capitalists, then the quantity of circulating commodity-values would be the same and, other circumstances remaining equal, would require the same amount of money for circulation. The question in either case is therefore only: Where does the money come from which serves as the medium of exchange for this quantity of commodity-values? It is not at all: Where does the money come from which monetizes the surplus-value?" (ibid. p. 552). It comes, and this is the point, from the gold producer, or, in a regime of nonconvertibility, from the printing press of the central bank. We are talking about monetary *material* aren't we?

On the level of capital circulation, in order to be realized surplus value *must* be sold, that is, *acquired with incomes*. A commodity is not sold against a quantity of general equivalent money (be it gold or bank notes) but against a quantity of incomes. Even in a regime of nonconvertible money the object is still *incomes*, because in a regime of nonconvertibility like the present one, which does not have a problem of production of *commodity-money*, the question of the quantity of monetary incomes remains the same: *who* creates these incomes and, above all, to *whom* are these incomes paid?

The point that strikes me as truly fundamental is that in most cases analyses have been put forward *as though* the problem of the realization of surplus value were resolved by the functioning of the economic circuit described by Marx in volume II, that is, on the basis of his diagrams of reproduction; in other words, *as though* the problem of the Marxian criticism of Say's law, which as is well-known fixes the *identity* between supply and demand in monetary terms, were reduced to hoarding, to the suspension of the circulation of those incomes which, by subtracting them from the system, breaks the chain of transactions C-M-C'-M-C" and provokes an imbalance, a build-up of unsold commodities.

Even remaining, purely as a working hypothesis, within the sphere of simple circulation, Marx's criticism of Say's law is not sustainable today, at a level, that is, of development of the productive forces of monetary circulation (digitalization and globalization) such that the lack of income in any point of the circulation of values (owing to a savings, which is a form of hoarding) is *automatically* compensated for by the movement of savings from one part of the globe to another. But besides this fact, the important fact is that this criticism of the identity of Say's law cannot stand unless it *first* responds to the question of how surplus value is monetized in the circulation of *capital*.

In reality, Marx provides all the necessary requisites for developing a radical critique of Say's law, be it for going beyond the underconsumption thesis of Rosa Luxembourg or, even, beyond Keynes's thesis of the tendency toward the underemployment of productive resources. But on one condition: that one assumes that the imbalance is structural, in the sense that it is created in the production phase, revealing the impossibility of realizing the surplus value *on the sole basis of the salary incomes distributed at the beginning of the circuit of capitalist production.*

In the *Grundrisse*, Marx reflects on the question of the monetization of surplus value using simple numerical examples: "There remains a surplus value, an addition as such, newly created, of 20 thalers. This is *money*, posited as a negatively independent value against circulation. It cannot enter into circulation as a mere equivalent, in order to exchange for objects of mere consumption, since circulation is presupposed as constant" (Marx, p. 366).

Surplus value, Marx says in this citation, is money, *but not* general equivalent money. So what is it then? "*Money*, then, in so far as it now already *in itself* exists as capital, is therefore simply *a claim on future* (new) labour… As a claim, its material existence as money is irrelevant, and can be replaced by any other title. Like the creditor of the state, every capitalist with his newly gained value possesses a claim on future labour, and, by means of the appropriation of ongoing labour has already at the same time appropriated future labour." This means to posit "future labour as *wage labour*, as use value for capital." And, in confirmation of our thesis, there is no "*equivalent* on hand for the newly created value; its possibility only in new labour" (ibid., p. 367).

So, to tie things up, for the new value (20 thalers in his example) there is no amount of general equivalent money, there does not exist, that is, a quantity of monetary incomes that would permit the sale of these 20 thalers of value-commodities. But there does exist an income which functions, if spent to acquire the 20 thalers, as a claim on future labor; as, in other words, money capital that will command new labor.

To put it simply, "on a par with public credit" the money for the monetization of the surplus value exists, but the condition for its existence is not its material nature ("its material existence as money is indifferent") but rather its ability to function as a claim on future labor, *as a vehicle for the salarization of new labor*. Or better yet: as money that commands living labor, the *use value* of the work force.

To claim that the imbalance is structural does not mean that, historically, solutions have not been found to the problem of the conversion/realization of surplus value. It means that the solutions are, and this is the point, historical and as such that they call for the study of the social and institutional arrangements which from time to time have regularized the cycle or led to the eruption of crises.

We have known colonialism and imperialism, that is, the search for *external outlets* from the capitalist circuit in order to realize surplus value not realizable internally. We know that imperialism reached the point of granting poor countries outside of the circuit the credit, the purchasing power, necessary for the importation of surplus value not realizable inside the circuit of developed countries. The policy of multinational banks toward poor countries, widely recognized as the debt trap, corresponds exactly to this solution of the problem of the monetary realization of surplus value (see Vitale, 1998).

One crux of the capitalist economy is ensuring the *continuity* of accumulation. Every interruption constitutes a social and political risk for capital. That is why, historically, the imperialistic way of guaranteeing the continuity of capitalist accumulation presupposes the *destructuring* of the natural economies of countries outside the capitalist circuit. The destructuring of poor countries, but, without restructuring, in order to keep them in a *dependent* relationship, because if they were restructured the contradiction between unrealized surplus value would simply re-present itself on a larger scale. The function of the debt trap is exactly that: to preclude peripheral countries from freeing themselves from their dependence on center countries, maintaining them, however, in their condition as outlet markets for center countries. This means that there is no development without underdevelopment.

The other "solution" to the problem of monetizing surplus value is the welfare state, whose deficit spending has, so to speak, resolved *inside the circuit* what imperialism resolved outside the circuit. The creation of *additional incomes* necessary for the realization of surplus value which contribute, together with wages and salaries, to the formation of effective demand, is done, and can only be done, through *deficit* spending. The new income must be an additional income, created *ex nihilo*, which is paid back when the realized surplus value, and the reinvestment of the realized surplus value, broaden the tax base by increasing employment for salaried workers. That additional income comes back in the form of higher tax revenues, thus permitting the elimination of the initial deficit.

It is evident that this system functions by virtue of its *continuity*, its capacity to guarantee the *commensurability* of commodities in circulation. If it is interrupted, as it is in periods when investments in constant capital do not create jobs but eliminate them, it sets off a cumulative spiral of deficits. In fact, continuing to use public spending to create additional demand in order to ensure the continuity of the circuit, but with investments which do not broaden the employment base, undermines the usefulness of deficit spending as an economic instrument. But, and this is the essential point, it is undermined not so much because the investments in constant capital fail to create additional employment, but because the mass of the unemployed who, in a modern welfare state, are eligible for unemployment benefits, do not function as a (potentially) new or future work force.

Strictly speaking, and according to Marx's indications in the *Grundrisse*, the deficit can continue to grow, but on the essential condition that the money created *ex nihilo* function simultaneously as a means of monetizing surplus value and as a claim on *future* labor. If the unemployed proletarians do not respect the conditions posed by the capitalist welfare state, if they do not demonstrate their willingness to accept their fate as future wage workers, then you have a "taxpayer strike" against higher tax rates, which is usually followed by a series of measures designed to rationalize public spending in order to reestablish the capitalist command over the future of the no longer productively employed work force.

I think it is important to examine one further question. The economic circuit is nearly always considered (implicitly or explicitly) to be coincident with the *national* economy. Everything we have been saying, therefore, is valid within each single national economy and each national economy is in turn enlisted in a network of relationships with a multiplicity of other national economies. Taken together, these relationships make up the *international economy*.

Given that each national economy is monetized in terms of its own accounting unit (dollar, euro, yen, etc.), and given that for each national economic circuit, according to Say's law, the gross domestic product is equal to the sum total of internally redistributed incomes, it follows that exchanges between national economies *should* be carried out in a supranational accounting unit. In fact, where international transactions are executed with a national accounting unit, as in modern economies where 80% of international payments are effected in dollars (the international currency), the asymmetry between the national currency and its international utilization cannot but generate economic-financial imbalances on a global scale.

For this reason, there have been repeated attempts over the last several decades to put an end to global economic and monetary instability by returning to the old *gold standard* or, along the lines of Keynes at Bretton Woods, by establishing an immaterial supra-national currency similar to the Bancor proposed by Keynes at the 1944 conference. In both cases, the idea is to restabilize the symmetry between national economic circuits by establishing a vehicular currency that would allow exclusively for the exchange of nationally produced portions of value without modifying the exchange rates in favor of this or that nation.

In the Marxist tradition this vision of the economy and international transactions is clearly identifiable in the definition of money as the *universal equivalent* of commodities. This is a commercial definition of money that—as we have seen earlier with regard to the diagrams of reproduction—belongs to the sphere of simple circulation, the sphere in which the commodities that are exchanged through the mediation of money are *already produced* commodities, already containing a certain amount of socially necessary work. We know that Marx develops this form of money (*general* equivalent, as it pertains to the national economic circuit, and *universal* equivalent as it pertains to the global circulation of commodities) in the first section of the first book of *Capital*.

Actually, in Marx money is a *form of value*, in the sense that value is present in the double form of commodities and money. As a form of value, its essence is not at all reduced to the generally equivalent form, given that this latter is but *one of the many functions* of money (accounting unit, measure of value, means of exchange, means of payment, reserve of value, etc.). Money, in other words, is the form which value takes on in certain relationships of exchange between buyer and seller.

As a form of value, money is the *form of social cohesion* characteristic of modernity, that is, "a way of 'accounting' individuals and organizing them into groups and distinct territories, by means of a relationship between private and public. Because it is a social link, money is also (functionally) an instrument of trade, and object of accumulation or support of power; but to reduce it to these functions alone would mean leaving out the essential" (Boyer-Xambeau, M.T.et ak, Gillard, 1986, p.3).

For example, in the absolutely fundamental case of the exchange between capital and the work force, money is the form of a value which *does not exist as* an equivalent *in circulation*, but of a value which *will be produced* by living labor once the work force enters directly into the circuit of production under the command of capital. This means that the money with which the salary contract is stipulated does not have commodity-salary equivalents in circulation; it is, in other words, money created *ex nihilo*, a means of payment which becomes commodity when the work force ceases to be separated from capital and, by starting to produce value, also produces the commodities of the salary-basket.

This means no more and no less than that payment of the salary *does not* presuppose any amount of corresponding money-commodity, since it is the in *actu* living labor which produces its salary-commodities. The quantitative correspondence between money in circulation and gold held by the central bank is thus irrelevant if for some reason the accumulation of capital is not stopped. When, on the other hand, the circulation of values is interrupted and consequently there is hoarding on a social scale, then the quantitative distance between paper money and general equivalent reveals the qualitative distance between modality of accumulation and work force, between capital enhancement and self-enhancement of the work force.

If we define money as a form of value, a form containing a set of *functions* (among them the universal equivalent function), then it follows that the economic circuit can, or better *must* be analyzed from a global point of view. Global money is, after all, a form of *global value*, a form of value which is produced with the contribution of economies whose nationality is derived not from the economic dimension of the citizenry but from their political dimension.

This makes it easier to understand that odd statement by Marx: "The world market thus constitutes in turn, and together, the premise and the support of everything." The world market is a "premise" in the sense that the production of value is not national but worldwide, but at the same time the world market is "the support of everything" in the sense that the international division of labor and the hierarchical organization of exchange functions as the framework for the entire world market.

Within the worldwide form of value, the weight of the various functions of money will vary historically depending on whether international commerce (the exchange of already produced commodities) or the production of new value is preponderant. In the first case, the function of money as universal equivalent will have greater weight relative to the function of money as a means of payment; in the second case it will be the contrary. In both cases, however, the fundamental asymmetry is not that between national currency and its use on the international level, but rather that between the work force and its capitalistic utilization, between distributed salary (across the spectrum of national accounting units) and global surplus value.

It should be noted that even a "century before the emergence of issuing banks [therefore, in the sixteenth century], money was not limited to gold or silver but already formed a specific interplay between private practices and public prerogatives, *a process of sociality*. And the breakups of the late sixteenth century led to the first crisis of this modern money, showing the limitations of its as a social link" (*ibid.* p. 7). Already at the dawn of the modern monetary system, the existence of a plurality of regional-national accounting units means that monetary relationships are international *not* because they presuppose a crossing of borders, but because they convert different regional accounting units. In other words, the accounting unit does not define the nationality of the economic circuit, but holds within itself the *diversity of the global space of capital enhancement.*

The disproportion, typical of the monetary system dominated by the dollar, between the *national* accounting unit and the *international* means of payment, though on the one hand a consequence of the productive force of a certain *national-space* relative to the rest of the world, also reflects the need of the strongest economy to avoid the interruption of the process of production/circulation of value in one or more points on the world circuit.

Finally, we must take account of the fact that even in a regime of immaterial (nonconvertible) currency, the function of general equivalent money does not disappear with the disappearance of gold, but the universal equivalent is replaced by a combination of monetary functions or systems which, from time to time, can function as a monetary support on a world scale (for example, a system of fixed exchange rates, or floating exchange rates, of strong currencies, "top-rated" bonds, etc.).

The Rationality of the Cyclical Form

"Let's imagine a primitive community of fishermen. The only consumer good: fish; the only productive activity: fishing. The tribe decides to reduce its consumption in order to free up a *surplus* to be used to improve its fishing equipment and, as a consequence, its productivity, with an aim to producing more fish later on. For this purpose, it decides to take a few men off the fishing detail and puts them to work making pirogues. From there a reduction in the consumption of consumer goods, an increase in investment, a decline in the production of consumer goods and a simultaneous increase in the production of means of production" (Arrighi, 1974).

What is the "moral" of this hypothetical community? It's this: that sector I, the production of capital goods, never grows independently of sector II, the production of consumer goods. Or better it does something even more important: it grows in proportion to the decline in the sector that produces consumer goods. This community not only *can* but *must* make the two sectors vary in inverse proportion, the one against the other. This is the necessary condition for maintaining its equilibrium. This is in conformity with the two quantities in play, because they are the only components of a given total quantity, which is the *social potential* of production and, consequently, they cannot but vary in inverse proportion, the one against the other.

"Now let's imagine that some private entrepreneurs intervene, invading the community and taking in hand, by privatizing them, all of its economic activities. The fundamental equation is reversed: no private entrepreneur will increase the production of pirogues at precisely the time that fish consumption is falling, nor will he cut back on production when fish consumption rises. For those who now hold the reigns of economic decision-making, the incentive to investment is directly proportional to consumption" (*ibid*, pp. 380–81).

In a certain sense, capitalists are induced to acting in an inopportune manner: to invest when—following the absorption by end consumers of a larger part of the social product—the means for investment are becoming scarce; to disinvest, or to slow down the rate of investment, when—following a drop in end consumption—the means for investment are overabundant. It is in this form, on the level of the realization (sale) of the product, that the fundamental contradiction between social production and the private appropriation of wealth is revealed. This is what determines the instrumental imbalance in the capitalist mode of production, which is to say, of the market economy.

At this point it is fair to ask why, *despite* this imbalance, despite the fundamental contradiction between the private interest of the entrepreneurs and the objective conditions of social production, the free market system is not immediately and permanently blocked. The answer is that, in the *capitalist* community "of fishermen," the manufacture of pirogues and the production-consumption of fish can rise and fall simultaneously (thus making the sum total of pirogues and fish *elastic*), but only on one condition: that there exists in the community a reserve of unemployed workers and/or a reserve of means of production which can be mobilized or demobilized according to the circumstances.

If, for example, the economic system is open then, besides the internal reserve of productive forces, we have the contribution of external productive forces in the form of capital and workers. This contribution adds a *supplementary elasticity* to the effective potential of social production, that is, to the sum total of the productive forces actually put to work at the time under consideration. It is this reserve, internal and/or external, and therefore this very tendency of the system toward underemployment, which allows the capitalist economy to function according to a logic which is the reverse of the logic of the community of fishermen: instead of consuming as an increasing function of production capacity and as a decreasing function of investment, it produces and invests as an *increasing* function of added consumption (consumption, it must be recalled, which is only apparently unproductive, since it actually carries with it the *productive future of the work-force*). Here lies, in effect, the secret behind the miracle of the thirty golden years: the substantial *salary increases* in that period functioned as an *engine* of economic growth and not as a brake!

So, if we start from the presupposition that there is a basic structural imbalance in the operation of the economic circuit, and this is the precise result of P (production, supply) *greater than* R (income, consumption), then *overtrading*, in so far as it is the creation of income *in addition to that created directly inside the circuit*, allows us to explain the oscillatory dynamics of expansion and recession: the cycle. *Overtrading does not send the circuit out of balance, on the contrary, it balances it dynamically.* As such, overtrading is additional income (created by means of credit granted to importing countries outside of the capitalist circuit or by means of public *deficit spending*) which brings overall income to the level which was known to classical and neoclassical economists as general equilibrium.

But it is a kind of additional income which is created *from outside the circuit*, which actively presupposes a consciousness of the *collective interest* of capital, an awareness owing to the fact that the economic circuit is, by nature, constituted by an assemblage of individual interests which, if they are not organized as a class, are unable to see beyond their own noses. In fact, each entrepreneur views the salaries paid to his own employees as a pure cost, and not as an element of final income which will allow him to sell his surplus value.

In the Fordist era, the driving force of *overtrading* was triggered by the *deficit spending* of the welfare state, together with the dynamics of international trade (exports toward peripheral countries in accordance with the logic of dependence). In that case, the business cycle was managed on the basis of the indications given by Keynes: the economic system having a tendency toward under-employment of productive forces, the creation of additional demand on the part of the welfare state, always however within an imperialist international context, transformed unemployed human resources into salaried work force. The Keynesian-Fordist business cycle, in other words, had a tendency toward full employment in center countries and toward destructuring *sans* restructuring in peripheral countries.

Within the Keynesian cycle the upper limit of expansion, the limit beyond which you enter into recession, was full employment. As the economy drew nearer to this limit, or rather as the growth rate of consumption gradually slowed, the growth rate of indebtedness (public and private) originated by *overtrading* revealed the approaching upper limit of the cycle, which unleashed the banks in a race, each against the others, to recover the loans granted during the expansion phase. This is how the expansion phase spilled over into the recessive phase: by turning off the faucets of overtrading, nonmonetizable surplus value, in the form of unsold goods, was left high and dry. A surplus value made up primarily, at least initially, of capital goods.

As in the Fordist era, the role of the welfare state in creating additional demand never succeeded in eliminating the role of peripheral countries as market outlets outside the imperialistic circuit (even where peripheral countries began to develop economically their dependence on center countries remained just as it had been), in the New Economy the financialization of the business cycle does not eliminate (though it certainly reduces them) the role of the welfare state and the world economy as devices for the monetization of surplus value.

The overtrading of financial markets, imprudently defined (in 1996, some four years prior to the beginning of the crash) by the Governor of the Federal Reserve as "irrational euphoria," no longer has as its upper limit the Fordist-Keynesian tendency toward full employment of generically-defined human resources but rather the tendency toward full employment of *cognitive human resources*. When the economy approaches the limit of the human capacity to absorb the supply of informational goods, financial overtrading, needed in the expansion phase to ensure the continuity of economic growth, ends up turning into a "preference for liquidity," hoarding on a worldwide scale, revealing a "digital cornucopia" of informational surplus value no longer monetarily absorbable by current demand. This is the beginning of the recessive crisis of the New Economy.

To return to Marx and the *Grundrisse*, the creation of money *ex nihilo* in its capacity as a *claim on future labor*, that is, as money capital which, *as such*, can very well be created independently of the amount of general equivalent money in circulation, comes to a halt as soon as *rigidity* develops in the process of conversion of generic human resources commanded by capital. The Fordist paradigm exploded when salary increases revealed, behind their *positive* economic function, their *negative*, so to speak, *political* function, their having become, that is, the vehicle for the growth of the opposing power of workers in the very gut of an expanding economy. The New Economy paradigm, on the other hand, goes into crisis when the modes of social wealth production themselves undermine the political control of the monetary authorities with regard to the creation of the (*necessary*) incomes for the monetization of surplus value, when *financial overtrading* undermines the autonomy of monetary regulation by the central banks (see Mayer, 2001).

It's hard to resist the temptation to compare the late 1990s fever for tech stocks to the Dutch tulip mania of the early 1600s. "The most spectacular, and certainly the most alarming of these speculative breakouts," writes Simon Schama, "was the great tulip mania of 1636–37. It has been the subject of much astonished and bemused writing, perhaps because of the apparent incongruousness between the banality of the flower and the extravagance of its treatment. Only a deeply bourgeois culture, it is implied, could possibly have selected the humble tulip—rather than, say, emeralds or Arabian stallions—as a speculative trophy. But there was noting suburban about tulips in the seventeenth century. They were, at least to begin with, exotic, alluring and even dangerous. It was precisely at the point that their rarity seemed capable of domestication for a mass market that the potential for runaway demand could be realized. It was this transformation from a connoisseur's specimen to a generally accessible commodity that made the mania possible" (Schama, 1987, pp. 350–351). Even though the historical explanation of the crisis of overproduction of the Dutch bulbs and the accompanying speculative bubble is still not entirely clear, it would seem to some observers that, behind the massive use of financial instruments such as *stock options*, there may be the aim of certain economic groups to prevent a growing number of people from entering a market which until then had been foreclosed to them—

just what happened at the moment in which tulips were transformed into standardized products accessible to all.

Over the course of the 1990s the new technologies represented the *general intellect* in its cooperative and liberating aspects (on this topic see the excellent historico-cultural reconstruction of the computer revolution by M. Revelli, *Oltre il Novecento, parte II, Il dilemma dell'uomo flessibile*), and, as exchange-traded securities, the *chance* to become rich. For lots of young people Silicon Valley actually worked as a place to emigrate to. They went there to test themselves, to put to work their own specific, singular cognitive-productive qualities. The "banality" of the computer, its being a force of *immediate* reticular cooperation, worked as a lever for a theoretically limitless production of immaterial goods. In a certain sense, the *general intellect* was imported "from outside" the economic circuit, a little like in the industrial era when immigrants were imported at times when, inside the capitalistic circuit, all of the unutilized productive resources had been employed and, politically, salaries couldn't go up anymore, even nominally.

The *standardization* of technological goods, which has transformed the financial markets into devices for the creation of incomes/returns on a (albeit inequitable) social scale, deserves some reflection. If in the New Economy, as Rifkin has said, "the temporary access to goods and services—in the form of leasing, renting and so on—becomes an ever more attractive alternative with respect to purchase and long-term possession" of commodities, whether they are consumer goods or capital goods (tangible or intangible) (Rifkin, 2000,, p.35); if new capitalist property takes the form of control over lifestyles (the product is no longer an expression of a lifestyle but, on the contrary, a lifestyle becomes the social representation of the product), then it follows that the commodification of cultural, sexual, economic, and ethnic differences in the workforce is based on the *necessary linguistic condition* of the workforce. Not this or that language or culture, but *language* in general, that is, the capacity to transform itself into lifestyles as commanded by the use/consumption of this or that commodity.

This idea allows us to understand the theory of *increasing returns* brought to the fore by the New Economy. An innovation, albeit banal or coincidental, could not spread cumulatively like an oil spill if the (linguistic) capacity to metabolize it socially did not already exist. "Them that has gets," says Brian Arthur, a complexity theorist at the Santa Fe Institute. Usually the first example used to explain the theory of increasing returns is the standard QWERTY keyboard common to all typewriters (the name is formed by the first six letters on the top row of the keyboard). "Is this the most functional way to arrange the letters on a typewriter keyboard? Certainly not. An engineer named Christopher Scholes designed the QWERTY layout in 1873 specifically to slow typists down; the typewriting machines of the day tended to jam if the typist went too fast. But then the Remington Sewing Machine Company mass-produced a typewriter using the QWERTY keyboard, which meant that lots of typists began to learn the system, which meant that other typewriter companies began to offer the QWERTY keyboard, which meant that still more typists began to learn it, et cetera, et cetera" (Waldrop, 1992, p. 114).

To make a profit, a company that produces intangible goods at marginal costs approaching zero has an absolute need to make its products accessible on a massive scale. The theory of increasing returns refers to *general* linguistic abilities (by *slowing down* the most competent typists, the QWERTY keyboard made it possible to "put to work" the linguistic abilities of the world population). But at the same time, increasing returns *presuppose* a monopoly on innovations, the ownership of intellectual property without which general linguistic ability can quickly turn into the mass appropriation of reproducible wealth. In other words, to ensure profits the linguistic labor of the abstract typist "who is in each of us" must become wage labor.

Since the early 1980s the number of patents granted by the U.S. government has doubled. In 1999 alone the number of patents came to 161,000. To defend themselves against competition, both domestic and foreign, like the Asian producers of semi-conductors, American technology companies have become increasingly aggressive. And the American Congress, by instituting a new court of appeal for patent applications in 1994, has accelerated the push for patent protection. Whereas in the Fordist era patents were considered primarily as tools in the hands of monopolistic companies, in the New Economy the patent has become the instrument for ensuring capitalistic control over the *general intellect*. The antitrust decision against Bill Gates revealed the political contradiction between the need to ensure profits through the legal protection of intellectual property and the need to ensure innovation by giving the widest possible berth to competition.

Hoarding and Multitude

Let's recapitulate what we've said so far about the rationality of the cyclical form.

The economic system can reproduce itself on condition that it be propelled by a set of driving forces that we have called *overtrading*. In the New Economy the financial markets have played a key role in the creation of additional incomes (*overtrading*), radically modifying the form of the business cycle on a global scale.

In the capitalist economy investments are only made in increasing function of final consumption, therefore—paradoxically —in decreasing function of savings. At a given level of employment this is a logical impossibility. It reflects the contradiction between the incentive to invest, which is directly proportional to consumption, and the material means of the investment, which are on the contrary inversely proportional to consumption. The system can resolve this contradiction by modifying the level of employment in the same direction as the expansion or contraction.

Thanks to *overtrading*, the business cycle maintains a state of unstable equilibrium. It moves in one direction or the other, it expands or contracts, contradicting its own logic: the development of productive forces (of the organic composition of capital).

The technological revolution that characterizes the New Economy has changed the nature of the business cycle in the sense that the facility of investment in high-tech (financialization, abundance of venture capital, low cost of money, influx of capital from the rest of the world, strong dollar, collective imagination, etc.), though it certainly energizes the expansive phase, runs up against a new saturation limit (new compared to the classic saturation limits determined by salaries, employment level, immigration). This new limit is the *capacity for absorption/consumption of new technology products for information.* In previous business cycles, the growth of sector I, producer of the means of production, was inhibited by the growing weakness of final consumption, weakness that increased as the threshold of full employment approached. In the new business cycle, investments in new technologies can grow beyond the threshold of full employment, both because the new technologies have decreasing costs and because the products of new technologies have increasing returns and cost margins equal to zero, and because the linguistic nature of the new technologies determines a potential market that is virtually infinite (just think of all the people still not connected to the net in developed countries not to mention those in emerging and poor countries). The threshold that marks the upper limit of the New Economy business cycle is no longer material consumption determined by the level of employment (that is, the capacity for final spending), but *immaterial consumption*, the amount of "time remaining" in a society in which the largest portion of time is spent trying to achieve an income for material consumption. An economy in which informational goods are strategic needs attention time.

Raising the threshold in order to generate more expansive force means *inventing a global welfare* in which the creation of incomes to employ unutilized human resources is aimed at *producing free time*, time of distraction from the real economy, antieconomic time. What the New Economy needs is antieconomic time.

The New Economy realizes it is approaching the upper limit (which marks the beginning of the recessive phase) when the relationship between the stock price and company earnings (*price/earnings ratio*) points to an average rate of profit for a number of years too high for the average investor. This is the moment in which the self-referentiality of the markets multiplies the risk of illiquidity on a social scale. This leads to an outbreak of (Marxian) hoarding, or of the (Keynesian) preference for liquidity, that is, abstention from investment. Notice that, in further support of the thesis of the structural imbalance between supply and demand, investors abstain from investment when the difficulty of realizing a profit has already become evident, which is to say when unsold inventories have already accumulated. It is not, at bottom, the preference for liquidity that breaks the equality between supply and demand. On the contrary, it is the existence of a disproportion between supply and demand that generates the preference for liquidity in the terminal phase of the business cycle. Indeed, the elimination of overtrading reveals the existence of an excess, of a surplus value, theoretically nonexistent if the cycle had developed on the basis of the equality of supply and demand. This is the reason that in the New Economy there is a relatively long period of time (almost a year) between the perception of an excessively high p/e ratio and the actual beginning of the recessive phase. The first to pay the consequences of a buyer's strike are those sectors that had pulled the p/e ratio up to its high level, which is to say, in the New Economy, shares of companies in the communications capital goods sector (industrial equipment including computers and peripherals, electronic equipment including telecommunications and semiconductors, communication services. In 2000 these three industrial sectors together generated 3.5% of all U.S. profit, but from the end of 1997 through the first six months of 2001 their profits increased by 70%).

The centrality and pervasiveness of the financial markets in the New Economy substantially changes the nature of hoarding. In a highly financialized economy the preference for liquidity, that is, the sale of securities in order to take possession of previously fixed money-capital, *cannot* be realized by everyone at the same time. To be able to sell there must be someone who is willing to buy. On a global scale this is logically, as well as actually, impossible. This "paradox of liquidity" reveals the contradiction between economic value and financial value: market securities are an abstraction of something quite concrete, that is, fixed physical capital that produces goods and services. The fixity of productive capital is a given that the liquidity of securities, the unfixity of liquid capital, cannot change. There is no global liquidity because, globally, the market is irremediably committed to productive capital. "Liquidity," as Orléan writes, "is only a process of re-allocation of the company property among investors" (Orléan, 1999, p. 47). The losers are only the investors without power, the shareholders who cannot exercise their power of ownership over the productive capital. Hoarding ultimately leads to a shifting of material wealth from the mass of small shareholders to the new owners of the productive capital.

Hoarding thus also reveals the contradiction between individual rationality and collective rationality. What is rational on the individual level (to sell when it is believed that a stock has reached its apex), is not rational on the collective level (if everyone sells at the same moment there are no possible buyers). With the preference for liquidity the social enactment of public opinion turns into its opposite, into the *rationality of the multitude*. This is a losing rationality as long as the weight of fixed physical capital continues to make hoarding a process of reallocation of private property. But the rationality of the multitude (to be understood as the exact opposite of the financial *community*), becomes *innovative* when the production of wealth is concentrated only in the *general intellect*, in the *cooperation of living labor* which has no fixed physical capital other than the bodies of the agents of the *general intellect* itself (in this sense the *Dot Com* enterprises are a prefiguration of the *general intellect* turned collective enterprise). In this case, hoarding means a preference for something still more abstract than liquidity, it means demand for wealth, for the various forms of wealth: the freedom of social cooperation among the multitude, the freedom of the languages that run through the multitude, the freedom of the singularities of which it is composed. And the multitude's ownership of its body.

Hoarding and Panic

Historically, panic has functioned as a factor of hoarding on a planetary scale. But, despite the gravity of the crises which for over a decade have punctuated the evolution of the New Economy, one cannot but be struck by the declining impact of the panic factor.

Let's ask ourselves then: in the era of the New Economy, what Pan, what goat-god of nature, provokes the experience of panic, the onset of powerful anxiety generated by a fear so unbearable as to impede the organization of thought and action, capable of depersonalizing, of inducing impersonal behavior and mass mimicry? What is the "raw nature" that produces, *brings to light*, the "all or nothing" instinct, that "liberates" latent anxiety? "If Pan is the god of nature 'in here,' then he is our instinct" (Hillman, 1972, p.28).

Already the fact that Pan, for all of his legendary "naturalness," is a creature that does not exist in the natural world (he is, in fact, half man, half animal), that is to say, a totally *imaginary* creature, allows us to define the "raw nature" within that nurtures our instinct as a *metaphor*. As Jung explains, if instinct acts *and* at the same time forms an image of its action, produces, that is, its representation, then the feeling of "being at the mercy of" the depersonalization which panic generates constitutes the experience of a synchronically primary *and* intelligent behavior. There is a method to our panic.

We arrived at this paradoxical conclusion by studying the genealogy of financial crises, particularly the crisis of 1929, as explosions of the same *rationality* of speculation, the activity which, according to Keynes, consists in predicting the psychology of the market, in "outwitting the crowd." "Knowing that our own individual judgment is worthless," writes Keynes, "we endeavor to fall back on the judgment of the rest of the world, which is perhaps better informed. That is, we endeavor to conform with the behavior of the majority or the average. The psychology of a society of individuals, each of whom is endeavoring to copy the others leads to what we may strictly term a *conventional* judgment" (Keynes, 1973, p.114).

The *mimetic relationship* between the individual economic actor and the others (the aggressive "crowd" of investors/speculators) has its rationality in everyone's lack of knowledge. When the conventional indicators, which represent the average values, no longer reflect the logic of the workings of the economic system, when the opacity typical of the financial markets induces behaviors whose rationality is now out of phase with respect to the economic transformation in progress, mimetic behavior intensifies the crisis, thus revealing the contradictory logic underlying the economic process, the immanence of the crisis within economic development. The functional mode of panic is thus a *necessary condition* of the panic attack.

As long as we can be confident that the convention, arbitrary as it is, will be maintained, mimetic behavior is completely rational. "But it is not surprising that a convention, so arbitrary in an absolute view of things, should have its weak points" (Keynes, 1973, p.153). The panic explosion, the frantic race to the banking windows to regain possession, in the form of money, of the property perceived to be "at risk," is nothing else than the revelation of the panicky nature of the capitalist mode of production, of its intrinsic precariousness. The panic demand for money reveals the contradictory nature of the market economy: everyone returns to his own property and, simultaneously, he finds himself closer to the others because of effects of mimesis, because of the contagion and the reactions it provokes (Orléan, 1988).

The violence of the crisis, far from reflecting the irrationality of the "raw nature" within us, represents the fear of the inadequacy of the conventions and the institutional powers in knowing how to manage the changed social conditions of economic development. At the same time, the "exuberant" utilization by individuals or groups of the ideas emerging from the ongoing processes of transformation represents the latent desire to be free from all authority, to be liberated from the slavery of the past. "Is not the Terror of 1793 both the apogee of holy terrors and the harbinger of their death? Although the religious spirit still inspires all the events and acts of the Revolution, it is also dying, as demonstrated by the failure of the revolutionary feast organized by Robespierre" (Depuy, 1991).

The ambiguity of meaning in the concept of panic, the confusion between true name and false alarm, led the catastrophe theorist, Colonel Chandessais, to conclude categorically that "panic does not exist." Even at Hiroshima "the panic that made some Japanese jump into a lake is dubious" (Jeudy, 1997). All that exists are images of panic and the fascination provoked by the images. The origin of panic always depends, therefore, on a *modality* of alarm and the *interpretation* of the danger signals. Therein resides the *linguistic dimension of panic*, its being a "play on words." Considered at one and the same time to be the essence of the Mass and the image of its dissolution, as the origin of the being and its destruction, panic is the image of the *disarticulation of language* and its representations. Much more than profuse sweating, pallor, palpitations, dyspnea, and tremors, being prey to panic means *being unable to speak*. The fear is so great that it cannot be identified with any object from which to defend oneself, a condition which amounts to *no longer being able to produce representations*.

The disarticulation of language defines the coordinates of the panic experience in post-Fordist society (Virno, 1994). This experience also defines "the raw nature"—the god Pan who, according to the Jungian principle of synchronicity, connects the nature within us to the nature "out there"—as a way in which the world in general manifests itself. But in post-Fordist society, the world in its entirety, the context in which every entity is located, all events happen, and all speech resounds, is inherently a *linguistic* world. Language, the communicative and discursive fabric which embraces the world in its entirety as one big text, is the "raw language" with which we perceive the material context and experience the world. Language, *in general*, language as *faculty* or capacity to communicate, is what we are afraid to lose. In the post-Fordist context, in which language has become in every respect an instrument of the production of commodities and, therefore, the *material* condition of our very lives, the loss of the ability to speak, of the "language capacity," means the loss of belonging in the world as such, the loss of what "communifies" the many who constitute the community.

Since panic manifests itself in the loss of the capacity to speak, as the disarticulation of language, the physical incapacity to name or recall objects (aphasia or dysphasia), it is the faculty of language, language as a possibility of existence which we are afraid to lose. The aphasic experience, described by Jakobson (1971) as "the evasion of identity toward contiguity," as escape from the referentiality of language to contextuality, involves the relationship between language and world. When one is prey to panic he flees to no place in particular, to wherever, looks for shelter in the world as a whole. It is this mass escape to a formless world that jams the escape routes, demonstrating how little room there is when everyone belongs to the same linguistic context, when everyone has the same fear of being deprived of the same property, of the same language faculty. As Virno has written, "the panic fear is not the consequence of a fracture between individual biography and the interpersonal powers that sustain society, but, on the contrary, it springs from the magnetic adherence of the individual to the *general intellect*. Or better, from an adherence which is magnetic because it is deprived of spatial regulation" (Virno, 1994, p. 74).

In a panic situation—a fire in a movie theater, for example— the other suddenly becomes a real enemy; amid the risk of being trampled, of suffocating, every movement of his becomes an attack on my body. As if to say that the *private* use of the *general intellect* clashes with its *social* nature, the individual body which incarnates the division of linguistic labor sees the body of the other as an obstacle. Only apparently was the movie theater the space in which the many were exercising their language faculty.

Catastrophe experts submit that the more people refuse to believe in the imminence of the danger, and don't want to abandon their own property, the more it is possible to prevent the eventuality of risk and, therefore, of a possible catastrophe. In an eminently linguistic context, in which one works by communicating, the resistance that prevents the eventuality of risk is possible if it is possible to distinguish false alarms from real ones. The capacity to interpret the indicators, the *benchmarks* which, in the form of simple numbers, synthesize a complex set of variables interpretable on the basis of a shared rationality, is possible only if the resistance of the individual is *at the same time* the resistance of the many, only if the interpretation of the warning signals of catastrophe happens through the use of the language that communifies and *preserves* the multitude.

In a context of high systemic risk (linguistic and global, such as the post-Fordist system of production and circulation of commodities), *linguistic resistance* is strong, rational, and independent from false signals if it succeeds in contesting the dominant language without in turn reproducing a totalizing language; if it functions as a "war machine" which does not reproduce in negative form what it is fighting against, the catastrophic homologation of individual actions, but rather the implosion of the realm of meanings, of equivalences and identities. The community as a people is catastrophic, mentally ill, the community as multitude is in good health "even if it all goes wrong" (Deleuze, 1993).

But how in a post-Fordist society, characterized by a high degree of systemic complexity which by definition the commonly used indicators fail to fully represent, can the rationality of mimetic behavior manage to protect the community of the multitude from the false alarms and the stereotypical representations of panic transmitted continually by the mass media? How can the multitude protect itself from panic when everything seems to contribute to the creation of the optimal conditions for mimetic behaviors which risk producing real and proper catastrophes?

This question should not be understood as an implicit denial of the history of social, cultural, economic, and ecological damage produced over the course of time by irresponsible political choices, *concrete* choices which have created and spread the feeling that an imminent disaster could destroy the world we live in (Davis, 1999). On the contrary, what we must do is demonstrate how it is possible to avoid the social injustice and the natural disorder within the very logic that turns anxiety into panic, the action of the multitude into uniforming behavior in itself catastrophic.

The Asian crisis, the millennium bug at the end of the 20th century, and the very crisis of the New Economy demonstrate that the scenarios of financial collapse and electronic catastrophe, transmitted repeatedly by the mass media, have not provoked panic behavior. For example, during the Asian crisis, analysts were surprised by the wisdom of millions of savers who, despite being bombarded by warning signals of systemic risk, did not stampede to withdraw their deposits from pension funds or mutual investment funds. The climate of catastrophe created by the millennium bug syndrome did not create that contagious behavior which could have legitimately been feared and which, independently of the falsity or reality of the danger, would *in fact* have provoked the catastrophe, made it inevitable, and certainly destructive of well-being.

The euphoria of the financial markets raises the specter of a worldwide financial crash. The financial-economic indicators and comparisons with the stock market performance in the 1920s justify the fear of a crash of epic proportions. In such situations, the reason of those who see increasing stock prices not as the reflection of the irrational exuberance of speculation, but as the real growth in social production, is not at all sufficient to protect us from the risk of catastrophe. You can never win against the crowd and examples of those who manage to win against the logic of "rational expectations" of the market are rare indeed.

The problem no longer even pertains to the relationship between objectivity and subjectivity, between analysis of the real economy and its corresponding financial system, on the one hand, and the change in the "semantics of risk," on the other. The social distribution of risk orientation, the addiction to risk of a monetary economy in which "growth without inflation" compels the diversion of capital directly to exchange-listed companies, makes it more and more difficult to distinguish with Luhmann (1996) between risk and danger, system and environment, transaction and observation. Those who expose themselves to the high degree of risk deriving from their own decision to invest in stocks, according to the sociology of Luhmannian risk, should react in a totally different way to the danger of financial loss resulting from the euphoria of the financial markets and the mimetic logic that sustains it. If this were the case, the maneuvers of the central bank aimed at reducing the dangers of a polluted stock market environment should help to reduce the propensity to risk of individual players in the stock market game.

The problem is that, even wishing to establish a different proportion between real wealth and financial wealth, an increase in interest rates on the part of the central bank doesn't seem to be enough to convince investors to change their minds, to shift their savings to less remunerative but safer securities. In order to establish the relative autonomy of the monetary authorities (that is, the State) the multitude must deploy itself against the *uniquity* of the monetary indicators. In order to "normalize" the markets, to regulate them from the celestial heights of the central authorities, it is necessary to *provoke* a catastrophe, generate a panic such that the behavior of the many becomes uniform, to transform the multitude into a people united by the same logic.

The *crisis of monetary sovereignty*, the inability of the central bank to affect monetary aggregates, does not exhaust the role of the State in its function as the legal money lender "of last resort," but it subsumes it to processes of financial gain, turning monetary policy into a dependent variable of the financial markets. The post-Fordist architecture of the production and exchange of wealth has constructed the *space* of the multitude in *language*. The multitude is the effigy of money, the form of its sovereignty. After having killed the god Pan, the multitude has to learn to protect itself from those momentary gods who, like little gremlins, haunt accidental events.

Scrapping and the General Intellect

On 7 August 2001 the *Financial Times* publishes an article by Richard Tomkins with a title recognized by now around the globe, *No logo*. For months, the book by Naomi Klein has been a world-wide bestseller, but the author is not cited by the newspaper's editorialist, as though the politics of the symbolic were considered a salient characteristic of the protest movement of the "people of Seattle." The aim of the *Financial Times*'s analysis is to demonstrate, on the basis of data published by *Business Week*, that the crisis/transformation of the New Economy is much more effective than any black-block protester smashing an ATM machine of some global bank. Of the 74 brands included in the 2000-2001 ratings, 41 have lost value and the overall loss amounts to 5%. Since March 2000, date of the start of the crisis, 49 billion dollars have gone up in smoke. The crash involves not only the icons of digital capitalism, such as Amazon.com, Dell, and Nokia, but also the logos of solid Old Economy companies like Coca-Cola (less 5%), McDonald's (less 9%), Gillette (less 12%), and Nike (less 5%).

In the 1990s, a crisis of symbolic capital (the value of the brand) of this size wasn't even imaginable. After the fall of the Berlin Wall the brands of American multinationals, viewed before then as forbidden fruit, had been under siege by millions of new consumers from the former socialist countries. But in the second half of the 1990s, the love affair with the symbols of global capitalism is showing visible signs of crisis. *Local* brands start doing better than global ones. Consumers and producers prefer the symbols of national businesses. Why sell our national heredity to the *Yankees*? In just a few years the effects of Americanization in the former socialist countries seem to reawaken a certain nationalist spirit. In 2000, the ten most publicized products in China, including Coca-Cola and Procter & Gamble, had local brands.

In other words, the logo seems bound to be localized. The multinationals are certainly not about to withdraw from emerging markets. Even if, in July, McDonald's decides to close 250 restaurants in emerging countries and Proctor & Gamble cuts back on its productive capacity abroad to concentrate on North America, the crisis of the global logo reflects a strategic rethinking similar to the one provoked by "Marlboro's black Friday" in 1993: "in the six years prior to 1993, Nike had gone from a $750 million company to a $4 billion one, and Phil Knight's Beaverton, Oregon emerged from the recession with profits 900 percent higher than when it began" (Klein, 1997, p.16). From that moment on, Klein says, the brand becomes a "cultural sponge, able to absorb from the environment and to remodel itself after it," to emancipate itself from the factory and from national borders in order to commodify desires, fantasies, lifestyles, to *capitalize the immaterial*.

The logo crisis of 2001 shows the increasing complexity of mass marketing. According to Martin Henley, president of a London market research company, "people don't want to be seen as 'normal'—everyone wants to be seen as an individual." The *individualization* of symbolic capital, *mass customization*, corresponds to the symbolic regionalization of the global economy. On the one hand, the annual growth in the supply of new products (in the U.S. alone in 2000 some 31,432 new products were launched) is such that symbolic capital is forced to develop "local" distribution strategies. On the other hand, this microphysics of symbolic capital is the result of the *singularization* of the citizen-consumer, of his exodus from an overly collective imagination, from forms of life that are overly global. Paradoxically, the localization/regionalization of branding signals a crisis of the communitarian imagination. The people of consumers, which in the 1990s was exploited globally by Nike's branding policy, has ended up turning into a multitude of resistances against the spiritualization of life forms.

The "no logo people" has been constituting itself with protest tactics against the privatization of public space, against the symbolic commodification effected by the multinational producers of consumer goods. The protests against the logo and against the world circuit of exploitation of the work force described by Klein have worked as a lever in the global growth of an "antiglobal" movement. For this reason, according to Luisa Muraro, the no logo of the movement refers to a politics "that does not limit itself to the economy nor does it attempt to correct the economy with rights, but it plays on desires and relationships, for a freer more personal way of living and living together." Global symbolic capital, by abandoning the macro level for the micro level of desires and the need for relationships, reveals not so much an (already consumed) awareness of the centrality of the consumer's "communicative-relational action" but rather the search for strategies for commodifying the imagination of the multitude.

The global crisis of the logo, in other words, suggests that it is on the terrain of the *political definition of the body* of the multitude that the future of the protest movement will be played out. What is the symbolic politics of a movement which, by criticizing the capitalistic use of the collective consciousness, has managed to become a global movement? What is the body of this movement which has organized itself and struggled concretely on the symbolic-linguistic level?

In an editorial with the cynically provocative title *Prologo*, which makes fun of the political fragility of the economic analyses of the *Financial Times* and of Naomi Klein, *The Economist* shows that it has a perfectly clear idea of what's at stake (8 September 2001). The logo is *power*, of the consumer and the producer, a power based on trust, fidelity, the loyalty of the consumer that capitalist businesses must conquer *by working* hard on the linguistic-communicative level. The power of the logo has literally *constituted* the space of the global economy, bringing manufactured commodities to unknown lands and so making them *known* to the wage laborers of the most developed economies. That is why, writes *The Economist*, with more than a little irony, *the protest against the logo* has allowed the antiglobalization protest movement to become known all over the world. As though to say that the power of the logo consists in its establishing a symmetrical—or worse *dialectical*—relationship between logo and no logo, between the power of capital and "globalization from below," between the *use value* of commodities and the living body of the movement (a problem about which Klein is politically aware and which looms in the background throughout the 500 pages of *No Logo*).

The limits of the antiglobal movement are, therefore, political, in the sense that, in trying to expand on the terrain of the symbolic politics of power, it has come up against the limits of its analysis of the workings of global capitalism. The global dimension of the antiglobal movement thus risks reducing itself to a protest movement, a movement that is by definition a minority movement precisely when it reaches its maximum degree of worldwide visibility, with its leaders caught up in a decidedly vacuous logic of negotiation. The wave of opening up (of the IMF, the WTO, national governments, the *Financial Times*, *The Economist*), the attempt to dialogue with the movement gets all tied up inside itself. *After* the G8 meeting in Genoa, the package of measures agreed upon by the IMF and the Argentine government, with the clauses ("democratically" proposed to the IMF by the Minister for the Economy Carvallo himself!) on *zero public deficit* and the transfer of tax revenues to local authorities, is *even more liberalist* than all of the "structural adjustment" measures imposed by the IMF on Asian or Latin American countries *before* the meeting in Genoa.

Our analysis of the genesis of the crisis of the New Economy allows us to identify the specific difference between capitalist globalization and the global protest movement. As we have tried to demonstrate, the New Economy has this peculiar element: it is a mode of production imbued with communication, by the *productive force* of language, both in the directly productive sphere of commodities and in the monetary and financial sphere. Therefore, it is within the linguistic coordinates of the New Economy's production and distribution that we must look for the contradictions and the forms of social conflict.

We have seen how the *attention economy* is the result of the growth rate of technological devices for information access and the need to accompany the supply of goods and services with devices that capture the attention of consumers. On the supply side, the New Economy is characterized by *increasing returns* by virtue of the intangibility and reproducibility of its capital goods (the infinite possibilities for cloning software, for example). On the side of demand for goods and services, however, attention (its allocation) has *decreasing returns*, because attention is a highly perishable and scarce commodity.

By attempting to overcome the resistance and the protest against Fordist-Taylorist work with management techniques for the "transfer of autonomy" and "personalization of work," the New Economy has given rise to reflective, cognitive, and communicative work, the *living* labor of the *general intellect*, centered on the linguistic cooperation of men and women, on the productive circulation of concepts and logical schemes inseparable from the living interaction of people. This transfer of autonomy and responsibility has led to an increase in the time dedicated to work and a reduction in the amount of attention time necessary to absorb the total supply of informational goods.

The *crisis of disproportion* between attention supply and demand is structural, given that this gap, besides being human, is *monetary* in nature. If in order to command attention it is necessary to invest increasingly more money (in addition to holding the intellectual property rights), in order to sell/realize the supply after eliminating the competition, it is necessary that, on the demand side, the side of the consumption of attention, there is sufficient disposable income to purchase the informational goods supplied by the market. But in the *attention economy*, income, instead of increasing, *diminishes* in direct proportion to the increase in the amount of time dedicated to work.

The disproportion between the supply of information and the demand for attention is a *capitalistic* contradiction, an internal contradiction of the value form, of its being simultaneously commodity and money, a commodity increasingly accompanied by information (necessary to carving out a market niche) and money-income increasingly distributed in such a way as to not increase effective demand. The financialization of the 1990s generated additional incomes but, beyond distributing them unequally, it created them by *destroying* occupational stability and salary regularity, thus helping to exacerbate the attention deficit of worker-consumers by forcing them to devote more attention to the search for work than to the consumption of intangible goods and services.

The condition imposed by the financial markets for the creation of financial gains has in fact been the promotion of *downsizing*, *reengineering, outsourcing*, and *mergers and acquisitions*, which have made the work force less secure by allocating more attention to the risk of losing exchange value than to the loss of use value of the work force. In the post-Fordist factory, the capital necessary to the production of informational goods has been subtracted from the remuneration of the qualities put to work by the work force. It has not been taken into account that the work force is not only a producer but a consumer of attention, not only salary cost but also income.

In the columns of the *Financial Times*, Dan Roberts asks himself what happened, how is it possible that intelligent people have got it so clamorously wrong. But the New Economy is not a historical oversight. Quite the contrary, it is the result of the determination with which capital has destroyed the Fordist factory, of the vampirization of cognitive labor. Capital has symbolically colonized public space and has symmetrically put to work the skills, know-how, knowledge, passion, affections, capacity to relate and to communicate of the work force.

The crisis of the New Economy has this peculiarity: scrapping electronic equipment does not destroy the knowledge that is incorporated in it. Today the *general intellect* is made up of *living* knowledge, of the capacity for cooperation which *remains in the body* of the multitude, even after all of the fixed capital has been disassembled in order to salvage some parts of it to sell on the used equipment market. Just as tomatoes were once destroyed in order to keep the price up and to reduce the wages of the work force, today the instruments of social communication are scrapped in order to devalue the body of the *general intellect*.

After the crisis, capital will again be forced to pursue the *general intellect*, its mobile body distributed throughout the entire planet. But in the meantime, in the time that remains before the capitalistic exit from the crisis, this multiple body has the chance to learn how to take care of itself, how to live well inside the temporal space that separates it from the euphoric irrationality of capital.

4

War and the Business Cycle

As I'm writing this, exactly six months after the September 11th terrorist attack on the twin towers and the Pentagon, all of the technical indicators are showing that the recession is over. If it really is over it will have been the shortest recession in the last fifty years. Nevertheless, it is not yet possible to tell if the recovery will be, as in the past, immediately followed by a relapse (giving the cycle the shape of a W), or if it will be a lasting recovery (in which case the cycle would have a V shape).

"The American economy has truly changed," says *Business Week*, with regard to this "surprisingly mild" recession (*The Surprise Economy*, 18 March 2002). Curiously, the analyses announcing the end of the crisis of the New Economy no longer take into consideration the fact that since September 11th there has been a war going on whose effects on the economy, though not immediately perceptible, must still be factored into the overall redefinition of the mid-to-long term macroeconomic and political context.

Yet, immediately following the terrorist attack there were a lot of observers who thought that, after years of private sector dominance over the public sector, the economy had to be restimulated with Keynesian type policies in sectors such as defense, airlines and insurance (two business sectors especially damaged by the attack), innovation (more public investment in research and development), finance (through improved regulation of the markets), and domestic security. The response of the U.S. government, although circumscribed to defense and the business sectors hardest hit by the attack, was certainly immediate and substantial. But today not even this return to "wartime Keynesianism" is taken into consideration to explain, at least in part, the end of the recession.

Let's see then what factors, according to current analyses, have contributed most to bringing the New Economy out of the crisis that began, let's remind ourselves, in the month of March 2000 with the crash of the Nasdaq, and was then marked by just one quarter of negative growth (the third quarter of 2001, during which U.S. GDP declined by 1.3%).

We have seen how the crisis manifested itself with an accumulation of unsold inventories, particularly (but not only) in the new technology sector. We have also seen how this crisis of overproduction, besides revealing a lack of effective (soluble) demand, also highlighted a new phenomenon, deeply rooted in the attention economy: in order to absorb the supply of goods and services, an economy innervated by communication technology needs consumers who have a large amount of *attention time*. Given that the New Economy is, in fact, an economy that consumes not only work time but also nonwork time or living time (in the sense that all of life is put to work), it follows that the crisis of the New Economy is determined by the contradiction between economic time and living time. In other words, the crisis explodes due to an "excess of economy," a disproportion between cyberspace and cybertime (to say it with Franco Berardi).

Faced with a decline in demand for investment goods (machines, new technologies), over the course of 2001, the U.S.

economy drastically reduced its unsold inventories. At Cisco Systems, for example—a symbol of the New Economy—inventories were reduced by 60% in a year—at 3M it was 57%, but inventories were reduced at the same pace throughout the economy. And when inventories are reduced the economy loses strength, in the sense that production declines and therefore so does employment. The reduction in accumulated inventories alone, in fact, subtracted one percentage point from the growth rate of U.S. GDP.

A reduction in inventories of this size was made possible by maintaining consumption, particularly the consumption of durable goods. The demand for automobiles and houses, and the persistence of buying power uneroded by inflation (whose permanent *structural* reduction, as we have seen, is a primary characteristic of the post-Fordist mode of production) have allowed the economy to hold up in a phase in which the crisis of the financial markets appeared to compromise any chance of recovery. In reality, it is precisely the crisis of the financial markets, which forced the Federal Reserve to cut interest rates 11 times over the course of 2001, that allowed a growing mass of people to go into debt (for example, by refinancing their mortgages) in order to maintain a stable level of consumption. In the expansion phase, financial gains from the stock market were overly concentrated among high-income classes, those with a low marginal propensity to consumption and who, therefore, do not contribute to keeping demand high in the recessive phase.

Besides consumption, the other factor which has played a positive role in ending the recession is *labor productivity*. During the last quarter of 2001 it grew by 5% (and at an average annual rate of 2.4%). Usually in recessions, productivity drops because of cuts in production, but not in this one. This is a very important fact because it means that during the recovery phase, that is, when it is time to build up new inventories after having exhausted the old ones, it will be possible to realize profits without raising prices on goods and services but rather, and here's the point, by just relying on higher labor productivity. Furthermore, with the risk of inflation now eliminated, the central bank can avoid raising the cost of money, it can continue, that is, to keep interest rates down in the face of a considerable increase in demand for credit from both business and household economies.

The unprecedented endurance of labor productivity during a recession is a decisive factor for understanding the logic of the business cycle of the New Economy. In part, we have already addressed this question earlier. The novelty is that labor productivity has increased in parallel with a decrease in profits (-20% in 2001), a combination never seen before. According to a study by the Conference Board, productivity gains in the United States are three times those of the European Union and involve all economic sectors, not only the information technology sector. Even those economists, such as Robert Gordon, who have been most critical of the New Economy are now convinced that since 1995 the American economy has really changed, that the New Economy cannot be reduced to a speculative bubble on the financial markets.

Productivity has been able to grow during the recession thanks to the *flexibility* of the work force and the *variability* of labor costs. While on the one hand, as was predictable, the variable portion of salaries, such as stock options and bonuses, has been strongly reduced, on the other hand, layoffs of temporary workers have made it possible to keep the overall cost of labor *below* the rate of increase in labor productivity. Although temps only account for 2% of salary costs in the U.S., the number of temp jobs lost in 2001 amounts to

30% of the total. It is precisely this reserve supply of flexible labor, coupled with the variability of total labor costs, that has made it possible to translate increases in productivity into increased real disposable income for those who have not lost their jobs.

Let's take a closer look. Over the course of 2001 the drastic drop in spending for capital goods (machines, new technologies) and the equally drastic reduction of unsold inventories should have provoked, were they to have remained in line with previous cycles, a wave of massive layoffs, a sharp drop in incomes and, consequently, a very serious recession. In reality, what we've seen, in a period of recession, is an unemployment rate that has, yes, increased, but not beyond 5.8% (well below the 10.8% of the 1981-82 recession). Moreover, thanks to the rise in productivity, production and real family incomes have increased even in the face of a decline in employment. And this is exactly what happened in 2001: the gross product of the New Economy grew by 0.4%, real wages increased by 2.5%, and consumer spending was up 3.1%.

To be sure, there are other factors which have helped the New Economy fend off the crisis of overproduction: the computerization of inventory monitoring systems; the reduction in life span of new technologies which has allowed the sector hardest hit by the crisis, the technology sector, to reduce its unsold inventories faster; the rapidity of the Fed in reducing interest rates, even before the recession was officially recognized.

The structural changes in the dynamics of the business cycle require us to take another look at the role of the flexible work force. It is the *general* flexibility of the work force that has ensured not only the growth of the New Economy but also its endurance in the recessive phase. Now, flexibility is a *collective good* that capital manages *privately*, hiring when the market is strong, firing when there is a drop in demand. Flexibility is a collective good because it is nothing other than the *general intellect* of living labor, intellect in *general*, or, as Paolo Virno has observed, "the most generic aptitudes of the mind: language faculties, disposition to learning, memory, ability to think abstractly and to correlate, an inclination to self-reflection" (Virno, 2002, p. 77). Without these general human qualities, without this simple *faculty* to think and to act, to modulate the "connection between one's own work and the tasks performed by others," *the flexibility of labor wouldn't even be imaginable*. The nonrecognition of the collective/public quality of the flexibility of the work force (of its *cooperative quality*) is what permits capital to *socialize the costs of crises while privatizing the benefits in the recovery phase*.

Another fundamental element in the analysis of the New Economy business cycle concerns the disproportion between *production time* and *work time*. "In post-Fordism," writes Virno, "'production time' includes nonwork time and the social cooperation that grows out of it. So I call 'production time' the indissoluble unity of compensated life and non-compensated life, overt social cooperation and covert social cooperation. Work time is only one component, and not necessarily the most important, of production time thus understood" (ibid. p. 74). To put it a little differently, in an economy based on the productive energy of communicative-relational action, we produce even when we watch television because we increase the number of viewers and therefore advertising revenue, etc.... "So then, it should be observed that in the post-Fordist era, surplus value is determined above all by the hiatus between a production time not computed as work time and work time in the proper sense of the term. What counts is no longer just the disparity, within work time, between necessary time and surplus time, but also (and perhaps more so) the disparity between production time (which includes within itself non-work, and its particular productivity) and work time" (ibid.).

In this disproportion, which redefines capital in Marxian terms as a *social relationship*, war plays a double role, one classical and the other consubstantial with the imperial form of post-Fordism.

First, in the recessive phase of the New Economy, war represents the occasion for absorbing a part of the *surplus* of informational goods produced in the "euphoric" phase of the New Economy. It is a fact that, after September 11th, increased spending on the military and for domestic security made it possible for the information technology sector to identify a new market outlet in the construction of a society centered on repressive surveillance and security measures. The digitalizing of surveillance and the destruction of the private sphere in the name of the struggle against terrorism makes it possible, in fact, to recycle a considerable part of the technological surplus otherwise destined to be scrapped. This broadening of the market for new technologies is not limited to the United States, but applies to the set of countries which, according to the "Bush doctrine" (elaborated by national security advisor Condoleeza Rice), demonstrate their determination in the fight against terrorism and therefore "deserve" economic aid from the United States. Economic aid, it must be recalled, *not* for eliminating the poverty in which anti-American terrorism ripens and is legitimized, as shown by the not very liberal imposition of tariff barriers to protect the U.S. steel industry or the shift toward Russia of the big oil alliance in order to reduce American dependence on OPEC (with disastrous consequences for the people of Saudi Arabia). Rather, the aid consists of direct foreign investment in the form of subcontracting (*outsourcing*) for the repression of local social protest movements.

Second, the war against terrorism being waged by the United States represents the *continuation of the New Economy by other means*. The New Economy took shape in an international context characterized by the end of the USSR which, against the background of the info-tech revolution, posed the problem of the form of world government. This gave rise to the use of term *Empire* to refer to the global politico-military regulation emerging form the *depolarization* process and the overcoming of the binary form of international equilibrium.

In the early 1990s the Empire presented itself as the *empire of disorder*, a set of particularly unpredictable explosive variables. In order to govern the empire of disorder on the basis of the technological superiority of the United States, a new *substantive* global strategy needed to be elaborated, one capable of going beyond the formal-institutional definition of regional alliances after the end of the Warsaw Pact. The collapse of the USSR, in fact, risked blurring the image of a world full of dangers. What was needed, therefore, were new conceptual instruments, *representations and paradigms* capable of accounting for the working logic of the world-system and its internal contradictions.

In 1993, the works of Alvin and Heidi Töffler (*Third Wave Information War*), Samuel Huntington (*Clash of Civilizations*), and Anthony Lake (*From Containment to Enlargement*) defined the conceptual bases of the American globalist strategy for the years to come. Despite the considerable differences among them, these theories share a series of aspects which revealed themselves to be especially significant during the Clinton presidency and, later, under the Bush administration. These common points are:

1) an "autistic" retreat to a nonstrategic, noninteractive consciousness of the Other, which derives from the annihilation of the global enemy and the disappearance of military bipolarism;

2) American leadership of the West and Western leadership of the world as a fundamental postulate based on the presupposed existence of irreversible inequalities within the global hierarchy;

3) the search for a principle of minimalist military intervention in the nonbipolar complexity of the world;

4) the definition of a *tyrannical* State as a State in which there is a politico-military dominance over the economic. The economic, especially the information economy, is the top priority for Töffler and Lake, while for Huntington economic predominance will be the outcome of the conflict of cultural identities, among which only the Judeo-Christian is nontyrannical.

It is on the basis of this American imperial consciousness that Clinton and Bush represent two different conjugations of the same problem: the global regulation of the New Economy. For the Clinton administration the expansion phase of the New Economy translated into the *enlargement* strategy proposed by Anthony Lake, or the spatial enlargement of the market economy, which includes debalkanization as the mode of military destruction of nation-state autonomy and the premise for the reunification of the Empire under the aegis of the technological superiority of the United States. It is a strategy that reveals a series of structural weaknesses in the paradigm of the New Economy in its international articulation. The financial crises in Southeast Asia (1997–98) and Russia (1998), with their repercussions within the United States (the near failure of the Long Term Capital

Management hedge fund), and the Argentine crisis reveal all of the difficulties involved in linearly universalizing a highly financialized market economy. The application of information technology by the American armed forces makes it possible to intervene virtually and promptly in theaters of conflict, confirming the superiority of the empire over the logic of the nation-state (and also over that of the United Nations which is still impregnated with the old logic). But this technological-military superiority is not enough to resolve the internal contradictions of the New Economy in its global deployment.

It is no coincidence that the transition from Clinton to Bush was marked by the *crisis* of the New Economy and by the immediate repercussions of this American crisis on a world scale. We have spoken about this at length in the preceding pages, underlining in particular how the force of the processes of financialization in promoting the digitalization of the economy, is based on the *asymmetry* of the financial markets, that is, on the attraction of the American financial markets, which thwarts any attempt at achieving economic autonomy by the rest of the world. It is enough to recall that Europe, despite outfitting itself with a regional currency like the Euro, has been unable to render itself monetarily independent from the United States because, in a system of global (and so also European) financialization, capital goes where the returns are greatest (that is, toward the United States).

In other words, the financialization of the New Economy is not only the lever of digital overproduction and, therefore, of economic cyclicity, but also the spur to reexamination of the Clintonian *enlargement* strategy. The strategy's greatest limitation consists in the fact that the universalization of the market economy is vitiated by contradictions *even stronger* than the contradiction between imperial expansionism and nation-States.

In order to assert itself, the superiority of the American digital economy (as theorized by Töffler) must somehow resolve a particular feature of the New Economy, which is to say, the *clanistic* and *criminal* nature of entrepreneurial behavior within the paradigm of the primacy of the economic. The stock market crisis had already highlighted the effects on millions of investors provoked by the "linguistic self-referentiality" typical of the workings of the financial markets. But it is especially the Enron scandal that demonstrates the clanist-mafioso relationship between economic growth (or between "irresponsible company") and the political regulation of governance.

Another contradiction peculiar to the New Economy which helped to accelerate the transition from Clinton to Bush regards oil. One place where economic *enlargement* ran aground in the United States was the California energy crisis. The liberalization of the energy market and, above all, the privatization of the production of energy revealed itself over the course of 2001 to be an outright *boomerang* for American consumers. In the wake of the California energy crisis, plans for expansion into central Asia for the construction of oil pipelines and the alliance between the U.S. and Russia are strategic measures thought to be essential for easing American dependence on Arab oil. It is likely that the timing of bin Laden's attack was determined by the awareness that these expansionist plans had already reached a point of no return.

It is within the contradictions of the New Economy as a form of political regulation of the Empire that we can explain Bush's choice to proclaim the crusade against bin Laden and against terrorism in general. From the perspective of ideological representation this constitutes the complete restoration of Huntington's conception, this time, however, in offensive rather than defensive terms, whose fundamental characteristics had already been part of the Clinton administration's strategy of enlargement. The superiority of Western civilization over Islam "justifies" the annihilation of the enemy as a way of ensuring the triumph of the New Economy. First and foremost, the decision to focus on the terrorism of the enemy of Western civilization, without ever invoking the economic and social contradictions of globalization, makes it possible to downplay the gravity of Western economic terrorism, the terrorism of Enron's management and of the current members of President Bush's cabinet.

A first, clear application of the Bush doctrine was the violent repression of the "no global" protest at the G8 conference in Genoa in July 2001. But Israel is the real laboratory for this doctrine in which expansionism and annihilation of the enemy are two sides of the same coin.

In conclusion, I think it is important to take a brief look at the concept of "biopolitics," which was used in the 1990s to describe the deployment of the Empire. The Empire, as we have said, needs peace in order to function, and therefore military intervention for humanitarian purposes represents the contrary of the government of naked life, the government of life as such. In light of what we have been saying, I find it difficult to maintain that the concept of biopolitics has actually been implemented. The problem is that this concept is imbued with powerful ambiguities that it would be well to point out.

Paolo Virno is perfectly correct when he writes "Biopolitics exists where the foremost priority, in immediate experience, is given to what belongs to the potential dimension of human existence: not the spoken word but the faculty to speak; not work actually done but the generic capacity to produce" (Virno, 2002, p.56). In biopolitics the living body of the work force is governed/regulated *exclusively* as a "substrate of a mere faculty," as a receptacle of the only thing that is truly important to capital, or the work force as a collection of the most diverse human faculties. "Life is placed at the center of politics whenever what is at stake is the intangible (and in and of itself not present) work force. For this, and only for this, it is legitimate to speak of biopolitics. The living body, which is the concern of the administrative apparatus of the State, is the tangible sign of a still unrealized power, the simulacrum of not-yet-objectified labor or, as Marx says with a lovely expression, of 'labor as subjectivity'" (ibid. p. 55).

This is a decisive specification for understanding the current phase of globalization and global *governance*. Biopolitics is not a prerogative of capitalist global government. During the years of the Clinton administration biopolitics was present only in a mystified form, always, however, within the strategy of economic enlargement on a global scale. It is, therefore, up to the protest movements to develop a *biopolitics from below*, a politics that takes care of the body of the multitude; that enables it to live for itself.

Bibliography

AGLIETTA M. (1995), *Macroéconomie fianciere*, La Decouverte, Paris.

AGLIETTA M., ORLÉAN A. (1998), *La monnaie souveraine*, Odile Jacob, Paris.

AGLIETTA M., LUNGHINI G. (2001), *Sul capitalismo contemporaneo*, Bollati Boringhieri, Turin.

AGOSTINELLI M. (1997), *Tempo e spazio nell'impresa postFordista*, manifestolibri, Rome.

ARRIGHI A. (1994), *The Long Twentieth Century: Money, Power, and the Origins of Our Times* Verso, New York-London.

ARRIGHI E. (1974), *Le profits et les crises*, Maspéro, Paris.

AUSTIN A.J. (1975), *How to Do Things With Words*, Harvard University Press, Cambridge. MA.

BAUMAN Z. (1998), *Globalization: The Human Consequences*, Columbia University Press, New York.

BERARDI F. (BIFO) (2001), *La fabbrica dell'infelicità*, DeriveApprodi, Rome.

BOLOGNA S., FUMAGALLI A. (eds.) (1997), *Il lavoro autonomo di seconda generazione*, Feltrinelli, Milan.

BOYER-XAMBEAU M., DELEPLACE G., GILLARD L. (1994), *Private Money and Public Currencies: The Sixteenth Century Challenge*, M.E. Sharpe, Armonk, New York.

BRONSON P. (2000), *The Nudist on the Late Shift and Other Tales of Silicon Valley*, Vintage, New York.

CEPII (1998), *L'économie mondiale 1999*, La Découverte, Paris.

CEPII (1998), *L'économie mondiale 2001*, La Découverte, Paris.

CHIAPELLO E., BOLTANSKI L. (1999), *Le nouvel esprit du capitalisme*, Gallimard, Paris.

CHICCHI F. (2001), *Derive sociali. Percarizzazione del lavoro, crisi del legame sociale e egemonia culturale del rischio*, Franco Angeli, Milan.

CHOMSKY N. (1998), *Profit Over People: Neoliberalism and Global Order*, Seven Stories Press, New York.

CILLARIO L., FINELLI R. (eds.) (1998), *Capitalismo e conoscenza. L'astrazione del lavoro nell'era telematica*, manifestolibri, Rome.

CIMATTI F. (2000a), *La scimmia che si parla*, manifestolibri, Rome.

CIMATTI F. (2000b), *Nel segno del cerchio*, manifestolibri, Rome.

COHEN D. (2002), *The Nature of Capitalism in the Information Age*, MIT Press, Cambridge, MA.

CORIAT B. (1993), *Ripensare l'organizzazione del lavoro*, Dedalo, Bari.

DAVENPORT T.H., BECK J.C. (2001), *The Attention Economy: Understanding the New Currency of Business*, Harvard University Press, Cambridge, MA.

DAVIS M. (1998), *Ecology of Fear: Los Angeles and the Imagination of Disaster*, Metropolitan Books, New York.

DECECCO M. (1998), *L'oro d'Europa*, Donzelli, Rome.

DELEUZE G. (1993), *Critique en clinique*, Ed. De Minuit, Paria.

DRUCKER P. (1976), *The Unseen Revolution: How Pension Fund Socialism Came to America*, Heinemann, London.

DEPUY J., *La panique*, Laboratoire Delagrange, Paris.

FIOCCO L. (1998), *Innovazione tecnologica e innovazione sociale. Le dinamiche del mutamento della società capitalistica*, Rubettino, Soveria Mannelli.

FUMAGALLI A. (ed.) (2001), *Finanza fai da te*, DeriveApprodi, Rome.

GALLI C. (2001), Spazi politici. *L'età moderna e l'età globale, il Mulino*, Bologna.

GALLINO L. (2001), *Globalizzazione e disuguglianze*, Laterza, Rome-Bari.

GILIOLI A., GILIOLI R. (2001), *Stress Economy*, Mondadori, Milan.

HABERMAS J. (1984), *The Theory of Communicative Action*, Beacon Press, Boston.

HABERMAS J. (2001), *The Postnational Constellation*, MIT Press, Cambridge, MA.

HARDT M., NEGRI, A. (2000), *Empire*, Harvard University Press, Cambridge, MA.

HARRISON B. (1994), *Lean and Mean: The Changing Landscape of Corporate Power in the Age of Flexibility*, Basic Books, New York.

HENWOOD D. (1997), *Wall Street*, Verso, New York-London.

HILLMAN J. (1972), *Pan and the Nightmare*, Spring Publications, New York.

HIRST P., THOMPSON G. (1997), *Globalization in Question: The International Economy and the Possibilities of Governance*, Polity Press, Cambridge.

JAKOBSON R. (1971), *Il farsi e disfarsi del linguaggio. Linguaggio infantile e afasia*, Einaudi, Turin.

JEUDY H.P. (1997), *Panico e catastrophe*, Costa&Nolan, Genoa.

KALDOR M. (1999), *New and Old Wars: Organized Violence in a Global Era*, Stanford University Press, Stanford, CA.

KEYNES J.M. (1937), *The General Theory of Employment*, "Quarterly Journal of Economic," now in *Collected Writings*, vol. XIV, London, 1973.

KEYNES J.M. (1973), "The General Theory of Employment, Interest and Money" in *Collected Writings*, vol. VII, London.

KLEIN N. (1997), *No Logo*, Knopf, New York.

KRUGMAN P. (2001), *Fuzzy Math: The Essential Guide to the Bush Tax Plan*, Norton, New York.

LESSARD B., BALDWIN S. (2000), *NetSlaves: True Tales of Working the Web*, McGraw-Hill, New York.

LORDON F. (2000), *Fonds de pension, piège à cons? Mirage de la democratie actionnariale*, Seuil, Paris.

LUHMANN N. (1996), *Risk: A Sociological Theory*, Aldine Transaction, Piscataway, N.J.

MAGRINI M. (1999), *La ricchezza digitale*, Il Sole 24Ore, Milan.

MANDEL M.J. (2000), *The Coming Internet Depression*, Basic Books, New York.

MAYER M. (2001), *The Fed*, The Free Press, New York.

MARAZZI C. (1998), *E il denaro va*, Bollati-Boringhieri—Edizioni Casagrande, Turin-Bellinzona.

MARAZZI C. (1999), *Il posto dei calzini*, Bollati-Boringhieri, Turin.

MARX K. (1998), *Capital*, GBR: ElecBook, London.

MARX K. (1993), *Grundrisse: Foundations of the Critique of Political Economy*, Penguin Classics, New York.

MAUGERI L. (2001), *Petrolio. Falsi miti, sceicchi e mercati che tengono in scacco il mondo*, Sperling & Kupfer, Milan.

MURARO L. (1992), *L'ordine simbolico della madre*, Editori Riunit, Rome.

MURARO L. (1998), *Maglia o uncinetto?*, manifestolibri, Rome.

NAPOLEONI C. (1976), *Valore*, ISEDI, Milan.

ORLÉAN A. (1988), *Per una teoria delle aspettative in condzioni di incertezza,* in *Moneta e produzione*, Einaudi, Turin.

ORLÉAN A. (1999), *Le pouvoir de la finance*, Odile Jacob, Paris.

PELLEREY R. (2000), *Il lavoro della parola, Linguaggi, poteri, tecnologie della comunicazione*, UTET, Turin.

RAMPINI F. (2000), *New Economy*, Laterza, Bari.

RAMPINI F. (2001), *Dall'euforia al crollo*, Laterza, Bari.

REVELLI M. (2001), *Oltre il novecento*, Einaudi, Turin.

RIFKIN J. (2000), *The Age of Access*, Tarcher, Los Angeles.

RULLIANI E., ROMANO L., (eds.) (1998), *Il postfordismo. Idee per il capitalismo prossimo venturo*, Etaslibri, Milan.

SASSEN S. (1994), *Cities in a World Economy*, Pine Forge Press, Thousand Oaks, CA.

SASSEN S. (1996), *Losing Control?*, Columbia University Press, New York.

SASSEN S. (1996), *Migranten, Siedler, Flüchtlinge. Von der Massenauswanderung zur Festung Europa*, Fischer Taschenbuch Verlag, Frankfurt am Main.

SCHAMA S. (1987), *The Embarrassment of Riches*, Knopf, New York.

SCHILLER D. (2000), *Digital Capitalism: Networking the Global Market System*, MIT Press, Cambridge, MA.

SHILLER R. (2000), *Irrational Exuberance*, Princeton University Press, Princeton.

SCHRAGE M. (2000), "Getting Beyond The Innovation Fetish," *Fortune*, November 13.

SEARLE J.R. (1983), *Intentionality: An Essay in the Philosophy of Mind*, Cambridge University Press, Cambridge.

SENNET R. (1998), *The Corrosion of Character: The Personal Consequences of Work in the New Capitalism*, Norton, New York.

SHEFRIN H. (2000), *Beyond Greed and Fear: Understanding Behavior Finance and the Psychology of Investing*, Harvard Business School Press, Boston.

SCHOR J. (1993), *The Overworked American: The Unexpected Decline of Leisure*, Basic Books, New York.

SOROS G. (1998), *The Crisis of Global Capitalism*, Little Brown, London-New York.

STRANGE S. (1998), *Mad Money: When Markets Outgrow Governments*, Manchester University Press, Manchester.

TIVEGNA M., CHIOFI G. (2000), *News e dinamica dei tassi di cambio, il Mulino*, Bologna.

TOMMATIS A. (1990), *L'oreille et la vie*, Laffront (I ed. 1977) Paris.

VELTZ P. (2000), *Le nouveau monde industriel*, Gallimard, Paris.

VIRNO P. (1994), *Mondanità. L'idea di mondo tra esperienza sensibile e sfera pubblicai*, manifestlibri, Rome.

VIRNO P. (1995), *Parole con parole. Poteri e limit del linguaggio*, Donzelli, Rome.

VIRNO P. (2001), *Lavoro e linguaggio*, in Zadini A., Fadini U., (eds.) *Lessico post-Fordista*, Feltrinelli, Milan.

VIRNO P. (2002), *Saggi di filosofia di linguaggio*, Ombre Corte, Verona.

VIRNO P. (2002), *Grammatica della multitudine*, DeriveApprodi, Rome.

VITALE A. (1998), *I paradigmi dello sviluppo. Le teorie della dipendenza, della regolazione e dell'economia-mondo*, Rubbettino, Soveria Mannelli.

WALDROP B. (1992), *Complexity: The Emerging Science at the Edge of Order and Chaos*, Simon and Schuster, New York.

WOODWARD B. (2000), *Maestro: Greenspan's Fed and the American Boom*, Simon and Schuster, New York.

ZANINI A., FADINI U. (eds.) (2001), *Lessico postfordista*, Feltrinelli, Milan.

ZARIFIAN P. (1995), *Le travail et l'énvénement*, L'Harmattan, Paris.

ZARIFIAN P. (1996), *Travail et communication*, PUF, Paris.

ZARIFIAN P. (2001), *Temps et modernité. Le Temps comme enjeu du monde moderne*, L'Harmattan, Paris.

SEMIOTEXT(E) Post-Political Politics

AUTONOMIA
Post-Political Politics
Edited by Sylvère Lotringer and Christian Marazzi

Semiotext(e) has reissued in book form its legendary magazine issue *Autonomia: Post-Political Politics*, originally published in New York in 1980. Edited by Sylvère Lotringer and Christian Marazzi with the direct participation of the main leaders and theorists of the Autonomist movement (including Antonio Negri, Mario Tronti, Franco Piperno, Oreste Scalzone, Paolo Virno, Sergio Bologna, and Franco Berardi), this volume is the only first-hand document and contemporaneous analysis that exists of the most innovative post-'68 radical movement in the West.

7 x 10 • 340 pages • ISBN-13: 978-1-58435-053-8 • $24.95

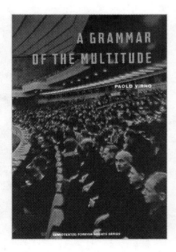

A GRAMMAR OF THE MULTITUDE
Paolo Virno, Translated by Isabella Bertoletti, James Cascaito, and Andrea Casson

Globalization is forcing us to rethink some of the categories—such as "the people"—that traditionally have been associated with the now eroding state. Italian political thinker Paolo Virno argues that the category of "multitude," elaborated by Spinoza and for the most part left fallow since the seventeenth century, is a far better tool to analyze contemporary issues than the Hobbesian concept of "people," favored by classical political philosophy.

Drawing from philosophy of language, political economics, and ethics, Virno shows that being foreign, "not-feeling-at-home-anywhere," is a condition that forces the multitude to place its trust in the intellect. In conclusion, Virno suggests that the metamorphosis of the social systems in the West during the last twenty years is leading to a paradoxical "Communism of the Capital."

6 x 9 • 120 pages • ISBN-13: 978-1-58435-021-7 • $14.95

MULTITUDE BETWEEN INNOVATION AND NEGATION
Paolo Virno, Translated by Isabella Bertoletti, James Cascaito, and Andrea Casson

Multitude between Innovation and Negation offers three essays that take the reader on a journey through the political philosophy of language.

"Wit and Innovative Action" explores the ambivalence inevitably arising when the semiotic and the semantic, grammar and experience, rule and regularity, and right and fact intersect. "Mirror Neurons, Linguistic Negation, and Mutual Recognition" examines the relationship of language and intersubjective empathy: without language, would human beings be able to recognize other members of their species? And finally, in "Multitude and Evil," Virno challenges the distinction between the state of nature and civil society and argues for a political institution that resembles language in its ability to be at once nature and history.

6 x 9 • 200 pages • 978-1-58435-050-7 • $14.95

THE PORCELAIN WORKSHOP
For a New Grammar of Politics
Antonio Negri, Translated by Noura Wedell

In 2004 and 2005, Antonio Negri held ten workshops at the Collège International de Philosophie in Paris to formulate a new political grammar of the postmodern. Biopolitics, biopowers, control, the multitude, people, war, borders, dependency and interdependency, state, nation, the common, difference, resistance, subjective rights, revolution, freedom, democracy: these are just a few of the themes Negri addressed in these experimental laboratories.

Postmodernity, Negri suggests, can be described as a "porcelain workshop": a delicate and fragile construction that could be destroyed through one clumsy act. Looking across twentieth century history, Negri warns that our inability to anticipate future developments has already placed coming generations in serious jeopardy.

6 x 9 • 224 pages • ISBN-13: 978-1-58435-056-9 • $17.95

Printed in the United States
By Bookmasters